Qualifikationsphase Sekundarstufe II

The New Pathway Advanced

Abi *kompakt*

Thematic Vocabulary • Important Facts • Relevant Skills

Herausgegeben und erarbeitet von:
Iris Edelbrock

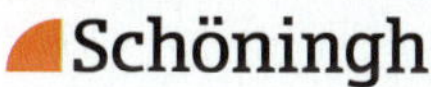

Picture acknowledgements

front cover: Thomas R. Greve; back cover: adapted from: www.eleanorjane.co.uk/blog/journal; S. 124: Europäische Union; S. 128: Klaus Hermsen; S. 130 li.: © The Art Archives; S. 134: Iris Edelbrock/Verlagsarchiv Schöningh; S. 135: Museum of American Folk Art, New York; S. 137: „Die Bevölkerung der USA an der Schwelle zum 21. Jahrhundert – Erste Ergebnisse der Volkszählung 2000". In: Petermanns Mitteilungen 145, Heft 5, 2001, S. 51–55. © Hans Dieter Laux und Günter Thieme; S. 138: © picture-alliance/dpa; S. 141: Picture-Alliance GmbH; S. 143: © picture-alliance/dpa; S. 145: SZ Photo/Melde Press; S. 148: World Economic Forum; S. 153: C. Walter Hodges, 1965; S.160, 170: Reinhild Kassing/Verlagsarchiv Schöningh; other illustrations: Verlagsarchiv Schöningh

www.schoeningh-schulbuch.de
Schöningh Verlag, Jühenplatz 1–3, 33098 Paderborn

Druck A 6 5 4 / Jahr 2017 16 15
Alle Drucke der Serie A sind im Unterricht parallel verwendbar.
Die letzte Zahl bezeichnet das Jahr dieses Druckes.

Umschlaggestaltung: Nora Krull, Bielefeld
Druck und Bindung: westermann druck GmbH, Braunschweig

ISBN 978-3-14-040155-5

Contents

Focus on Vocab

Focus on Facts

Focus on Skills

Focus on Language

Note: This * sign indicates that the word/term can be found in the *Glossary of Literary Terms* in your Student's Book, pp. 339 ff.

Great Britain – Between Imperial Heritage and Modernity

English word/phrase	Explanation in English	German equivalent and/or synonym(s)
Commonwealth		
allegiance to sb./sth. [əˈliːdʒəns]	loyalty to a leader	*Loyalität/Ergebenheit gegenüber jmd.*
to associate	to spend time or form a relationship with sb./sth.	*mit jdm. verkehren/umgehen;* to interact
association	relation	*Verhältnis, Umgang*
aspiration	ambition	*Bestreben, Ziel*
ceremonial position	a position that gives no real power	*zeremonielle/förmliche Position*
to be committed to sth.	willing to work very hard at sth.	*sich für etwas engagieren*
commitment	the hard work and loyalty that sb. gives sb./sth.	*Engagement, Leistungsbereitschaft*
to comprise sth.	to consist of sth.	*aus etwas bestehen*
core (values)	most important	*Kernwert, Grundwert*
criteria [kraɪˈtieriə]	standards that you use to judge sth.	*Kriterium, Maßstab*
declaration	an official statement	*(öffentliche) Erklärung, Bekanntgabe*
developing countries	poor countries that are trying to increase their industry and trade and improve life for their people	*Entwicklungsländer*
diversity [daɪˈvɜːsəti]	the fact of including many different types of people or things	*Vielfalt*
to establish sth.	to start sth.	*etwas aufbauen*

to face (a problem)	to deal with	*(ein Problem) erkennen, vor einem Problem stehen*
flow of (resources)	movement	*(Ressourcen-) Zufuhr, Fluss*
to foster (equality)	to encourage	*(Gleichheit) fördern*
to further (efforts)	to help sth. progress/ be successful	*(Mühen) unterstützen, fördern*
to frame (society)	to organize and develop sth.	*(eine Gesellschaft) bilden, formen, weiterentwickeln*
good governance	successful government	*erfolgreiche Regierung/ Politik*
guarantee [ˌgærən'tiː]	security of sth.	*Garantie, Sicherheit, Gewähr*
head of state	a leader or a person in charge of a state	*Staatsoberhaupt*
to share a common heritage	to have the same traditional beliefs, values, customs, etc.	*ein gemeinsames Erbe/ Kultur haben*
intergovernmental	between different governments	*zwischenstaatlich, international*
to issue ['ɪʃuː]	to officially make a statement	*Stellung beziehen*
legacy ['legəsi]	sth. that exists as a result of sth. that happened at an earlier time	*Erbe*
member state	a country/state that belongs to a community of different states	*Mitgliedsstaat*
to oppose	to disagree with	*ablehnen;* to dismiss
to participate	to take part in sth.	*(an etwas) teilnehmen*
(to hold) principles	moral rules or strong beliefs	*(an) Prinzipien (festhalten)*

prosperity	when people have money and everything that is needed for a good life	*Wohlstand, Hochkonjunktur*
to raise standards	to improve the quality or standard of sth.	*das Niveau heben*
representative position	a position in which sb. represents a state, a community, an interest, etc.	*repräsentative Position*
self-determination	the right of people to govern themselves	*Selbstbestimmung*
sovereign ['sɒvrɪn]	independent	*uneingeschränkt, souverän*
sovereign state	an independent state	*ein unabhängiger Staat*
sustained	continuing for a long time	*nachhaltig, dauerhaft*
urgency of sth. ['ɜːdʒənsi]	sth. that needs to be dealt with immediately	*Dringlichkeit*

English word/phrase	Explanation in English	German equivalent and/or synonym(s)
Multicultural Britain		
alien ['eɪlian]	foreigner; foreign	*Fremder; fremd*
alienation	the feeling of not being part of society or a group	*Entfremdung*
to apply for (a visa)	to make a formal request for sth.	*einen Antrag stellen auf*
application	a formal request for sth.	*Antrag*
to appreciate sth. [a'priːʃieɪt]	to understand how good/useful sb./sth. is	*etwas anerkennen, schätzen*

asylum seeker [ə'saɪlem 'siːkə(r)]	sb. who leaves their own country because they are in danger, esp. for political reasons, and who asks the government of another country to allow them to live there	*Asylbewerber*
citizen	a member of a state	*Staatsbürger*
citizenship	the legal right of belonging to a particular country	*Staatsbürgerschaft*
community	the people who live in the same area, town, etc.	*Gemeinde, Gemeinschaft*
to conflict with sb./ sth.	to disagree or argue with sb. about sth.	*mit jdm. wegen etwas im Konflikt liegen*
cultural clash	the difference and conflict that exists between cultures	*Zusammenprall der Kulturen*
(racial) discrimination	the practice of treating people differently from others in an unfair way because of their ethnicity	*(rassistische) Diskriminierung*
emigrant	someone who leaves their own country to live in another	*Aussiedler, Emigrant*
to emigrate	to leave the own country in order to live in another	*auswandern, emigrieren*
emigration	the process of leaving the own country in order to live in another	*Auswanderung, Emigration*

hospitable [hɒ'spɪtəbl]	friendly and welcoming to visitors	*gastfreundlich*
hospitality	friendly behaviour towards visitors	*Gastfreundschaft*
(public) housing	here: the houses or conditions that people live in	*Behausung, Lebensumstand*
identity-crisis	a feeling of uncertainty of who you really are and what your purpose is	*Identitätskrise*
to immerse (into a culture)	to adopt the customs and beliefs of a culture; to adjust to a culture	*eintauchen, einfließen*
immigrant	someone who enters another country to live there permanently	*Einwanderer, Immigrant*
to immigrate	to come into a country in order to live there permanently	*einwandern, immigrieren*
immigration	the process of entering another country in order to live there permanently	*Einwanderung, Immigration*
immigration control	the place at an airport, sea port etc. where officials check the documents of everyone entering the country	*Grenzkontrolle, Einwanderungskontrolle*
to integrate, integration	to become part of a group or society and be accepted by them, or to help someone do this	*integrieren, Integration*

interracial marriage	marriage between people of different ethnicities	*gemischtrassige Ehe*
minority	a small group of people or things within a much larger group	*Minderheit*
labour shortage	a situation in which there is not enough work	*Mangel an Arbeit*
the middle class	a social group typical of people who are educated and work in professional jobs	*die Mittelklasse/ Mittelschicht*
nationhood	the state of being a nation	*Nationalstaatlichkeit*
race relations	the relations between people of different races/ethnicity	*Beziehungen zwischen den Rassen*
refugee ['refju'dʒi]	someone who has been forced to leave a country , esp. during a war, or for political or religious reasons	*Flüchtling*
resident	sb. who lives or stays in a particular place	*Anwohner*
to settle (in a place)	to go to live in a new place, and stay there for a long time	*sich eingewöhnen/ niederlassen (in/an einen/einem Ort)*
temporary (stay)	a stay continuing for only a limited period of time	*befristeter Aufenthalt*
Western values	the beliefs, traditions, customs etc. of the Western world	*westliche Werte*

English word/phrase	Explanation in English	German equivalent and/or synonym(s)
Constitution/independence/treaties		
to administer	to manage the work or money of a company or organization	*verwalten*
administration	the activities that are involved in managing the work of a company or organization	*Verwaltung*
in accordance with the law	according to a rule	*gesetzesgemäß*
act	a law that has been officially accepted	*Gesetz*
to assess sth.	to make a judgement about sb./sth.	*etwas einschätzen/beurteilen*
bill	a written proposal for a new law that is brought to a parliament to be discussed	*Gesetzesentwurf*
charter/carta	a statement of the principles, duties and purposes of an organization	*Charta, Satzung*
compulsory	sth. must be done because it is the law or because sb. in authority orders you to	*verpflichtend*
to confirm	to show that sth. is definitely true	*bestätigen, akzeptieren;* to certify
confirmation	a statement, document etc. that says that sth. is definitely true	*Bestätigung*

constitutional document	an officially/a legally accepted document	*verfassungsmäßiges Dokument*
constitutional law	a law that is related to/based on the constitution of a country	*Verfassungsrecht*
constitutional monarchy	a country ruled by a king or queen whose power is limited by a constitution	*konstitutionelle Monarchie*
cooperation	when you work with sb. to achieve sth. that you both want	*Kooperation, Zusammenarbeit*
to deny sth. to sb.	to refuse to allow someone to have or do sth.	*jdm. etwas verweigern/ vorenthalten*
to be deprived of sth.	not having the things that are necessary for a comfortable or happy life	*sozial benachteiligt sein*
despot ['despɒt]	tyrant	*Despot, Tyrann*
Dominion	a country belonging to the British Empire or Commonwealth	*Dominion (selbstständiges Land des Commonwealth)*
to enjoy sth.	here: to have a particular ability or advantage	*befähigt/begünstigt sein etwas zu tun*
to be exiled ['eksaɪld, 'egzaɪld]	to be forced to leave your country	*ins Exil gehen*
to grant sth.	to admit that sth. is true	*etwas zugeben;* to admit
guarantee [ˌgærən'tiː]	security of sth.	*Garantie, Sicherheit, Gewähr*

Habeas Corpus (Act) [ˌheɪbiəs ˈkɔːpəs]	a law which says that a person can only be kept in prison following a court's decision	*Habeaskorpusakte (engl. Staatsgrundgesetz zum Schutz der persönlichen Freiheit; Haftbefehl)*
mutual (agreement)	when two or more people both agree to sth.	*gegenseitig*
to negotiate	to discuss sth. in order to reach an agreement, esp. in business or politics	*verhandeln*
negotiation	official discussions between the representatives of opposing groups who are trying to reach an agreement	*Verhandlung*
petition [pəˈtɪʃn]	an official letter to a law court asking for a legal case to be considered	*Petition, Antrag*
to proclaim sth.	to say officially that sth. important is true	*etwas (öffentlich) verkünden*
to request sth. from sb.	to ask sb. for sth. in a polite or formal way	*fordern*
subject	citizen	*Staatsbürger*

English word/phrase	Explanation in English	German equivalent and/or synonym(s)
	Historical development	
ancient [ˈeɪnʃənt]	very old	*uralt*
combat mission	fighting, especially during a war	*Kampfeinsatz*
to come into existence	to start being	*beginnen zu existieren*

collapse of sth.	the end of sb./sth.	*Zusammenbruch, Konkurs*
(political) crisis (pl. crises)	a (political) situation in which there are a lot of problems that must be dealt with quickly so that the situation does not get worse	*(politische) Krise*
to defeat sb./sth.	to win a victory over sb. in a war, fight, etc.	*jmd. in etwas schlagen/besiegen*
defeat of sb./sth.	to lose a battle against sb. in a war, competition, game etc.	*Niederlage gegenüber jdm./etwas*
formation of sth.	creation of sth.	*Bildung von etwas*
to found sth.	to build or establish sth.	*etwas gründen*
foundation of sth.	the establishment of sth.	*Gründung von etwas*
to invade	to enter a country/an area using military force in order to control it	*einmarschieren*
invasion of (a country)	when the army of one country enters another country by force, in order to take control of it	*Einmarsch in (ein Land)*
to join (a union)	to become a member of a group/an organization	*(einer Vereinigung) beitreten*
(historical) landmark	one of the most important events/changes or discover-ies	*(historisches) Wahrzeichen*
modernity [məˈdɜːnəti]	the quality of being modern	*Moderne, Modernität*

occupation of sth.	when a large group of people enter a place and take control of it, esp. by military force	*Belagerung*
to occupy	to enter a place in a large group and keep control of it	*belagern*
phenomenon [fə'nɒmɪnən]	sth. that happens or exists in society, science or nature, especially sth. that is studied because it is difficult to understand	*Phänomen*
(leading) power	a country that is strong and important and can influence events, or that has a lot of military strength	*(führende) Macht*
prehistory	the time in history before everything was written down	*Prähistorie, Vorgeschichte*
to rebel [rɪ'bel]	to oppose or fight against people in authority or against an idea or a situation which you do not agree with	*sich auflehnen, rebellieren*
rebellion [rɪ'beljən]	an organized attempt to change the government or leader of a country, using violence	*Rebellion, Widerstand*
to recapture sth. from sb.	to win back sth. that you already had in the past, for example a country or territory	*zurückerobern*

revolt [rɪ'vəʊlt]	strong and often violent action by a lot of people against their ruler or government	*Aufstand*
to revolt against sb./sth.	to oppose or fight against people in authority or against an idea or a situation which you do not agree with	*gegen etw./jdn. rebellieren*
tribal ['traɪbl]	relating to with a tribe or tribes	*Stammes-*
tribe	a social group consisting of people of the same race who have the same beliefs, customs, language etc., and usually live in one particular area ruled by their leader	*(Volks-) Stamm*

English word/phrase	Explanation in English	German equivalent and/or synonym(s)
	The British Empire	
administration	the activities that are involved in managing the work of a company or organization	*Verwaltung*
administrator	sb. whose job involves managing a company or organization	*Verwalter*
civil servant	sb. employed in the civil service	*Beamte(r)*
defence	protection	*Schutz, Verteidigung*

diplomacy [dɪˈpləʊməsi]	the job or quality of managing the relationships between countries	*Diplomatie, Verhandlungsgeschick*
emperor/empress	the man who is the ruler of an empire	*Kaiser(in)*
to establish sth.	to found sth.	*etwas bilden/aufbauen*
to expand	to become larger in size, number or amount	*expandieren, sich vergrößern*
expansion	growth	*Expansion, Wachstum*
fall	loss of power, failure	*Sturz, Umsturz*
foreign policy	involving or dealing with other countries	*Auslandspolitik*
to found sth.	to start sth.	*etwas beginnen/gründen*
foundation of sth.	the act of starting sth.	*Gründung*
to gain independence	to become independent	*(an) Unabhängigkeit gewinnen*
to grant sb. independence	to allow sb. to act on their own	*jmd. Unabhängigkeit bewilligen*
imperialism	a political system in which one country rules a lot of other countries	*Imperialismus*
indigenous [ɪnˈdɪdʒənəs]	native people who have always lived in a place	*einheimisch*
to be loyal to sb.	to support sb.	*jdm. treu sein*
maharaja [ˌmɒːhəˈrɑːdʒə]	an Indian prince or king	*Maharadscha*
overseas	to or in a foreign country that is across the sea	*Übersee*

(policy of) imperialism	a political system in which one country rules many other countries	*imperialistische Politik*
to possess sth.	to own sth.	*etwas besitzen*
possession	sth. that you have owned or obtained from somewhere	*Besitz;* property
Raj [rɑːdʒ]	British rule in India	*Britische Kolonialzeit in Indien*
to reign	to rule a nation as their king, queen or emperor	*regieren*
rise	the achievement of importance, power or control etc.	*Aufstieg*
rule	to have the official power to control a country	*Herrschaft*
self-government	a country or organization that is controlled by its own members	*Selbstverwaltung*
sovereignty ['sɒvrənti]	complete freedom and power to govern	*Eigenstaatlichkeit, höchste Gewalt*
subject	citizen	*Staatsbürger*
superiority of sb.	the quality of being better, more skilful, powerful etc. than other people or things	*Überlegenheit*
viceroy ['vaɪsrɔɪ]	a man who was sent by a king or queen in the past to rule another country	*Vizekönig*

English word/phrase	Explanation in English	German equivalent and/or synonym(s)
	Colonization	
the acquisition of colonies [ˌækwɪ'ziʃn]	here: the act of getting land	*Aneignung von Land/Fläche*
to civilize sb.	to improve a society so that it is more organized and developed	*jdn. zivilisieren, jdm. Manieren beibringen*
to claim a territory	to conquer a territory	*ein Territorium erobern/in Anspruch nehmen*
colonial power	when a powerful country rules many weaker ones, and establishes its own trade an society there	*Kolonialmacht*
to colonize	to establish political control over another country, and send your citizens there to settle	*kolonisieren, besiedeln*
colonization [ˌkɒlənaɪ'zeɪʃn]	the act of establishing political control over another country and sending your citizens there to settle	*Kolonisierung, Besiedlung*
colony	a country or area that is under the political control of a more powerful country, usually one that is far away	*Kolonie*
colonist	sb. who settles in a new colony	*Kolonist, Siedler*
to gain control over sb.	to obtain or achieve sb. you want or need	*Kontrolle über jdn. erlangen*

to conquer ['kɒŋkə(r)]	to take control of a country by fighting	*erobern*
conqueror	a person (often an army) who fights to take control of a country	*Eroberer*
conquest	the act of taking control of a country	*Eroberung, Sieg*
to decolonize sb.	to make a former colony politically independent	*jdn. entkolonialisieren/ in die Unabhängigkeit entlassen*
to discover	if sb. discovers a new place, they are the first persons to find it	*entdecken*
discovery	the act of discovering sth.	*Entdeckung*
to divide sth. up	to separate sth. into parts and share them between people	*etwas aufteilen*
to explore	to travel to or around a place in order to learn about it	*erforschen*
exploration	the act of travelling through a place in order to find out about it	*Erforschung, Erkundung*
to invade	to enter a country using military force in order to take control of it	*einmarschieren*
invasion [ɪn'veɪʒn]	the act of invading a country	*Einmarsch*

mother country	the country where sb. or sb.'s family were born (implies a feeling of strong emotional connection)	*Herkunftsland*
native	sb. who lives in a place all the time or has lived there a long time	*Ureinwohner*
negotiations	diplomatic talks to reach an agreement	*Verhandlungen*
policy	a way of doing sth. that has been officially agreed and chosen by a political party	*Politik, Strategie*
postcolonial	later than or after colonialism	*postkolonial*
to settle	to go to a place where no people have lived permanently before and start to live there	*(be-)siedeln*
settlement	when a lot of people move to a place in order to live there, esp. in a place where not many people have lived before	*Siedeln, Besiedlung*

English word/phrase	Explanation in English	German equivalent and/or synonym(s)
	Trade	
to benefit from sth.	to have advantage from sth.	*von etw. profitieren*
benefit	advantage	*Profit, Vorteil*
commerce	trade	*Handel*

economic power	a country that is economically strong and important and can influence events, or that has a lot of military strength	*Wirtschaftskraft, Wirtschaftsmacht*
(economic) suprema-cy [suːˈpreməsi]	the position in which a country/an economy is more powerful or advanced than others	*Übermacht, Überle-genheit*
to export sth. [ɪkˈspɔːt]	export of goods	*etwas exportieren*
to import sth.	to bring a product from one country into another so that it can be sold there	*etwas importieren*
import of goods	goods that are brought from one country into another so that they can be sold there	*Warenimport/einfuhr*
industrialized country	a country that has a lot of factories, etc.	*Industrieland*
Industrial Revolution	the period in the 18th and 19th centuries in Europe and the USA when machines were invented and the first factories were established	*Industrielle Revolution*
to manufacture sth.	to produce sth.	*etwas herstellen*
to provide sth.	to make sth. available	*zur Verfügung stellen*
raw [rɔː] **materials**	natural substances that are used in manufacturing goods	*Rohstoffe*

(natural) resources [rɪ'sɔːs]	soil, minerals, forests, water and energy sources	*natürliche Ressourcen*
to run sth. for profit	to do sth. because you want to make money with it	*etwas führen/machen für Profit*
secure markets	safe markets	*sichere Märkte*
slavery/slave trade	the system of having slaves/the buying and selling of slaves, esp. Africans who were taken to America	*Sklaverei/Sklavenhan-del*
taxation	the system of charging taxes	*Besteuerung*
to trade	to buy and sell goods	*handeln*
trading post/trading station	a place where people can buy and exchange goods	*Handelsniederlassung/ Handelsstation*
trade route [treid ruːt]	a way across land or sea used by traders	*Handelsweg*
trading company	business that buys and sells goods, esp. internationally	*Handelsgesellschaft*
transatlantic trade	trade/business invol-ving countries on both sides of the Atlantic	*transatlantischer Handel*
transportation network	a system of roads/ channels/railroads to transport goods	*Transport-Netzwerk*
triangular trade [traɪ'æŋgjələ(r)]	trade involving three continents: Europe, Africa and America	*atlantischer Dreiecks-handel*
wealth	a large amount of money etc. that a person or country owns	*Reichtum*

America – Still Dreaming?

English word/phrase	Explanation in English	German equivalent and/or synonym(s)
	US history	
to abolish sth. [ə'bɒlɪʃ]	to officially end a law, a system	*etwas abschaffen*
abolition of sth. [ˌæbə'lɪʃn]	the official end of a law or system	*Abschaffung*
to become independent from sb./sth.	to be one's own master	*von jdm./etw. unabhängig werden*
independence	political freedom from control by the government of another country	*Unabhängigkeit*
civil rights movement	citizens who fight for the rights that each person has in a society, whatever their race, sex or religion	*Bürgerrechtsbewegung*
discrimination	the practice of treating a person or group differently from another in an unfair way	*Diskriminierung*
to emerge	to appear; to begin to be known	*auftreten, hervortreten*
to escape persecution	to get free from persecution	*einer Verfolgung entgehen; fliehen*
to explore	to travel to or around a place in order to learn about it	*erschließen*
exploration	the act of travelling through a place in order to find out about it	*Erschließung*

to found sth.	to start sth., e.g. an organization, a company etc.	*etwas gründen*
Founding Fathers	sb. who begins sth., e.g. a new way of thinking (here: Thomas Jefferson, Benjamin Franklin, George Washington)	*Gründungsväter*
the Frontier ['frʌntɪə(r)]	the border between settled/civilized and unsettled/uncivilized country	*das Grenzland*
to gain independence	to become independent	*Unabhängigkeit erlangen*
interventionism	the policy of intervening in the affairs of another sovereign state	*Interventionismus*
isolationism	the policy of nonparticipation in international economic and political relations	*Isolation, Isolationismus*
non-violence	without violent actions; the act of doing sth. peacefully	*Gewaltlosigkeit*
pilgrim	a religious person who travels a long way to a holy place	*Pilger*
plantation	here: settlement	*Ansiedlung*
prejudice ['predʒudɪs]	an unreasonable dislike and distrust of people who are different	*Vorurteil*
to be prejudiced	having an unreasonable dislike of sb. or sth., mostly because of foreignness	*voreingenommen sein*

protest movement	a large group of people who come together to publicly express disapproval or opposition to sth.	*Protestbewegung*
purchase ['pɜːtʃəs]	sth. you buy	*Ankauf, Erwerb*
Puritan ['pjʊərɪtən]	a member of a Protestant religious in the 16th and 17th centuries, who believed in a simple and modest way of life and religious worship	*Puritaner(in)*
racial segregation	when people of different races are kept apart so that they live, work or study separately	*Rassentrennung*
to rebel [rɪ'bel]	to oppose or fight against people in authority or against an idea or a situation which you do not agree with	*rebellieren*
rebellion [rɪ'beljən]	an organized attempt to change the government or leader of a country, using violence	*Rebellion, Aufstand*
to run (a colony)	to be in charge of sth.	*(eine Kolonie) besitzen, betreiben*
to set up	(a contract) to arrange	*etw. einrichten/ aufbauen*
subject *(fml.)*	here: citizen	*Staatsbürger*
trading post	a place where people can buy and exchange goods in a country area	*Handelsstützpunkt*

tyranny ['tɪrəni]	government by a ruler who has complete power	*Tyrannei, Gewaltherrschaft*

English word/phrase	Explanation in English	German equivalent and/or synonym(s)
Politics/constitution		
administration	government, organization	*Regierung, Verwaltung*
(a nation's) affairs	public or political events/activities	*Angelegenheiten*
(to come to an) agreement	a decision or arrangement, often formal and written, between two or more groups or people	*sich einigen*
amendment	a change to a law that is still being discussed	*Zusatz (zur Verfassung)*
to amend a bill	to make changes to a (draft) law	*eine Gesetzesvorlage/ein Gesetz ändern*
appointment	the act of choosing sb. for a position or job	*Ernennung*
article	paragraph (of a law)	*Paragraph, Artikel*
to carry out a policy	to practise a policy	*eine Politik ausüben*
civil servant	someone employed in the civil service	*Beamter*
to confirm sth.	to say that sth. is definitely true	*bestätigen*
Constitution	a set of basic laws and principles that a country or organization is governed by	*Verfassung*
decision-making	the process of making important decisions	*Entscheidungsfindung*

to declare sth. unconstitutional	to say officially that sth. is not allowed by the constitution	*etwas für verfassungswidrig erklären*
domestic policy	the internal policy of a country without involving other countries	*Innenpolitik*
to draw up a bill	to carefully think about and design a bill	*ein Gesetz entwerfen*
to ensure (a right)	to make certain that sth. will happen properly	*zusichern;* to assure
foreign policy	involving or dealing with other countries	*Außenpolitik*
to form a government	to establish a government	*eine Regierung bilden*
to set up a government	to organize/arrange a government	*eine Regierung aufstellen*
to govern	to rule	*regieren*
grass roots (democracy)	the ordinary people rather than the rulers	*Basis, das Volk*
Head of State	the main representative of a country, such as a king, queen etc.	*Staatsoberhaupt*
to interfere with sth.	to prevent sth. from happening the way that it was planned	*sich einmischen*
to issue (a document)	to publish (a document)	*(ein Dokument) ausstellen, veröffentlichen*
party	here: a political organization which you can vote for in elections	*Partei*

policy	a set of ideas of what to do in particular situations that has been agreed officially by a government or a political party	*eine bestimmte Politik*
politician [ˌpɒləˈtɪʃn]	sb. who works in politics, especially an elected member of the government	*Politiker*
political [pəˈlɪtɪkl]	relating to governmental actions or people	*politisch*
to be politically impartial	not involved in politics	*unparteiisch sein*
to ratify a treaty	to make a treaty official by signing it	*einen Vertrag unterzeichnen*
reunification	to join the parts of sth. together again, esp. a country that was divided	*Wiedervereinigung*

English word/phrase	Explanation in English	German equivalent and/or synonym(s)
Beliefs/values		
achievement	sth. important that you succeed in doing by your own efforts	*Errungenschaft*
authority [ɔːθɒrəti]	the power you have because of your official position	*Autorität, Amtsgewalt*
cultural patterns/ habits	cultural ideas/ behaviour	*kulturelle Muster/ Gewohnheiten*
divine providence	coming from or relating to god	*göttliche Vorsehung*

to be equal to sb./sth.	to have the same rights as sb. else	*gleichberechtigt/ gleichgestellt sein*
equality [i'kwɒləti]	a situation in which people have the same rights, advantages etc.	*Gleichheit, Gleichberechtigung*
rags-to-riches	becoming very rich after starting life very poor	*vom Tellerwäscher zum Millionär*
God's chosen people	the believe to be particularly chosen and privileged by God	*Gottes auserwähltes Volk*
heterogenous society [ˌhetərə'dʒiːniəs]	a very diverse society	*verschiedenartige, breit gefächerte Gesellschaft*
to identify with sb./ sth.	to feel sympathy for sb./sth. or be able to share their feelings	*sich mit jdm./etw. identifizieren*
identification [aɪˌdentɪfɪ'keɪʃn]	a strong feeling of sympathy and similarity with sb.	*Identifikation*
inalienable/unalienable rights [ɪn'eɪlɪənəbl]	rights that cannot be taken from you	*unveräußerlich*
individuality [ˌɪndɪˌvɪdʒu'æləti]	the qualities that make sb. or sth. different from other things or people	*Individualität*
Manifest Destiny ['mænɪfest 'destəni]	the belief that the US people had the right and the duty to take land in North America from other people, because this was God's plan	*offensichtliche Bestimmung (amerik. Doktrin des 19. Jahrhunderts; göttlicher Auftrag zur Expansion)*
Melting Pot	a place where people from different races, cultures etc. live together and assimilate/adapt to each other	*Schmelztigel (der Kulturen)*

national anthem	the official song of a nation that is sung or played on public occasions	*Nationalhymne*
national pride	being proud of having a particular nationality	*Nationalstolz*
to offer an opportunity to sb.	to give sb. a chance to do sth.	*jdm. eine Gelegenheit bieten*
patriotism ['peɪtriətɪzəm]	when you love your country and are proud of it	*Patriotismus*
(to be) patriotic	having or expressing a great love of your country	*patriotisch (sein)*
prosperity	wealth	*Reichtum, Wohlstand*
Pursuit of Happiness [pə'sjuːt]	when sb. tries constantly to reach his personal goals and to live out your dreams	*Streben nach Glück, existentieller Sicherheit, Zufriedenheit*
religious tolerance [rɪ'lɪdʒəs 'tɒlərəns]	no discrimination of people from different religions and beliefs	*religiöse Toleranz*
self-improvement	the process of trying to become a better and happier person	*(selbstständige) Weiterbildung*
a set of ideas/values	a group of …	*Ideen-/Werteansammlung*
thrift	the habit of saving money and living economically	*Wirtschaftlichkeit, Sparsamkeit*
unlimited/limitless possibilities	endless opportunities and possibilities	*unbegrenzte/begrenzte Möglichkeiten*

English word/phrase	Explanation in English	German equivalent and/or synonym(s)
	Immigration/minorities	
alien	a person who is not a citizen of the country in which they live and work	*Fremde/r;* foreigner
to assimilate/ assimilation	to become a part of a country/community	*anpassen/Anpassung*
border control	measures taken to prevent illegal immigrants from entering a country	*Grenzkontrolle*
citizen	a person who has the legal right to belong to a particular country	*Staatsbürger*
descendant	sb. who is related to a person or family that lived a long time ago	*Nachkomme*
to emigrate (from)	to leave the own country in order to live in another	*auswandern*
emigration	the process of leaving the own country in order to live in another	*Emigration, Auswanderung*
ethnic	connected with a nation, race or people that share certain cultural traditions	*ethnisch*
ethnicity	the fact of belonging to a particular race or people/culture	*Ethnizität, Volkszugehörigkeit*
illegal alien	an illegal immigrant	*illegaler Einwanderer*
to immigrate (to) ['ɪmɪgreɪt]	to come into a country in order to live there permanently	*immigrieren, einwandern*

immigration control	the place where the passports and other documents of the people coming into the country are checked	*Einwanderungskontrolle*
(cultural) interaction	the act of communicating with sb. (from a different culture)	*(kulturelle) Interaktion*
multi-ethnic	involving or including different races/ people/cultures	*Vielvölker-*
naturalization	to become a citizen of a particular country	*Einbürgerung*
to be processed through sth.	to be moved forward from one checkpoint to the next	*durchgereicht/ durchgeschickt werden*
to take an oath of allegiance	a formal and very serious promise	*den Treueeid schwören*

English word/phrase	Explanation in English	German equivalent and/or synonym(s)
	Economy	
bankruptcy	the state of being unable to pay your debts	*Pleite*
to go bankrupt	to become officially unable to pay your debts	*Pleite gehen;* to go bust
capacity for sth. [kə'pæsəti]	the amount of space for sth.	*Kapazität für etwas*
capitalism ['kæpɪtəlɪzəm]	an economic and political system in which businesses belong mostly to private owners, not to the government	*Kapitalismus*

capitalist ['kæpɪtəlɪst]	sb. who owns or controls a lot of money and lends it to businesses, banks etc. to produce more wealth	*Kapitalist*
commerce	trade	*Handel*
to drop	to fall to a lower level or amount	*fallen, einbrechen*
drop	reduction	*Absturz, Abfall*
financial recession	a difficult time when there is less business activity, trade, etc. in a country	*finanzielle Rezession, Flaute*
hire and fire policy	to employ and dismiss people in quick succession	*Einstellen und Feuern von Beschäftigten*
homeowner(s)	people that own their home	*Hauseigentümer*
to launch a business	to start a business	*ein Geschäft abschließen/initiieren*
to be low-income	to be below an acceptable or usual level or quality of income	*geringverdienend sein*
ownership society	a society in which the possession of goods is very important	*Eigentumsgesellschaft*
real estate ['riːəl ɪ'steɪt] (*US*)	property in the form of land and houses	*Grundbesitz*
to regenerate [rɪ'dʒenəreɪt] (*fml.*)	to make sth. develop and grow strong again	*erneuern, umgestalten*
to subsidize ['sʌbsɪdaɪz]	if a government subsidizes a company, activity etc., it pays parts of its costs	*subventionieren*

subsidy ['sʌbsədi]	money that is paid by a government or organization to make prices lower and reduce the cost of producing goods	*Subvention*
to tax sb.	to pay an amount of money to the government according to your income, property etc.	*jdn./etwas besteuern*
taxation	money that has to be paid as taxes	*Besteuerung*
tax system	the system of charging taxes in a country	*Steuersystem*
upward mobility	the act of moving up through the social classes and becoming richer	*sozialer Aufstieg*
wealth [welθ]	a large amount of money etc. that a person or country owns	*Wohlstand;* prosperity
to be wealthy	to have a lot of property, money etc.	*wohlhabend sein;* prosperous

English word/phrase	Explanation in English	German equivalent and/or synonym(s)
Crises/war/poverty		
to accomplish a mission	to succeed in doing sth.	*eine Mission erfüllen*
challenge	sth. that tests strength, skill or ability	*Herausforderung*
combat	fighting, esp. during a war	*Kampf, Gefecht*

civil war	a war in which opposing groups of people from the same country fight each other in order to gain political control	*Bürgerkrieg*
crisis (crises) ['kraɪsɪs]	situation(s) in which there are a lot of problems that must be dealt with quickly so that it cannot get any worse	*Krise (Krisen)*
to declare war on sb.	to start a war against someone	*jdm. den Krieg erklären*
the (Great) Depression	the world economic crisis during the 1930s	*Weltwirtschaftskrise*
to fall into poverty	to become poor	*in Armut abstürzen*
to invade	to enter a country using military force in order to control it	*eindringen, überfallen*
invasion of a country	when the army of one country enters another country by force, in order to take control of it	*Überfall, Einmarsch in ein Land*
living standard	the level of comfort and the amount of money that people have	*Lebensstandard*
to occupy ['ɒkjupaɪ]	to enter a place in a large group and keep control of it	*belagern, besetzen*
occupant	member of the occupying force	*Besatzer*

occupation of ['ɒkju'peɪʃn]	when a large group of people enter a place and take control of it, esp. by military force	*Besatzung*
pre-military training	training that people get before joining the army	*militäre Vorbereitung, Training*
to recruit sb. [rɪ'kruːt]	to hire sb.	*jmd. rekrutieren/ einstellen*
social benefits	money provided by the government to people who are not able to work	*Sozialhilfe*
social ranking	related to the social classes people belong to	*soziale Rangordnung*
welfare (state)	a system in which the government provides money, free medical care etc. for people who are unemployed or not able to work	*Wohlfahrtsstaat*
to withdraw	to stop taking part in an activity	*sich zurückziehen*
withdrawal	the act of moving an army, weapons etc. away from the area where they were fighting	*Rückzug*

English word/phrase	Explanation in English	German equivalent and/or synonym(s)
Minorities (from *Pathway, Einführungsphase*)		
anti-discrimination legislation	laws against discrimination	*Gesetzgebung gegen Diskriminierung/ ungerechte Behandlung*

to assimilate/ assimilation	to become a part of a country/community	*sich anpassen/ Anpassung*
census ['sensəs]	the process of officially counting a country's population	*Volkszählung*
to conform to sth.	to obey a rule, to agree with	*sich (einer Meinung/ einem Vorschlag etc.) anschließen*
to contribute to sth.	to give sth. or help sb.	*zu etwas beitragen, helfen*
to decline	to become smaller, fewer, weaker	*weniger werden, abnehmen (in Menge);* to decrease
descendant	a person's descend-ants are their children, their children's children and all persons who live after them who are related to them	*Nachkomme;* relative
to be descended from sb.	to be related to sb. who lived a long time ago	*von jdm. abstammen*
to discriminate against sb.	to treat one person worse/better than another in an unfair way	*jdn. unfair behandeln, diskriminieren*
distinct from sth./sb.	clearly different	*unterschiedlich*
distinctive	characteristic	*typisch, bezeichnend*
diversity ['daɪ'vɜːsɪti]	variety	*Vielfalt*
equality	the fact of being equal in rights, status, advantages, etc.	*Gleichheit (gleiche Rechte haben), gleichberechtigt sein*

ethnic	connected with a nation, race or people that share certain cultural traditions	*Volks-*
ethnicity	the fact of belonging to a particular race	*Volkszugehörigkeit*
foreign-born	born in a different country from the one you live in	*im Ausland geboren, ausländischer Herkunft*
harassment	the act of annoying or worrying sb. by putting pressure on them or doing or saying unpleasant things to them	*Schikane*
(cultural/ethnic) heritage	the history and traditions that a country has had for many years and that have become an important part of its character	*(kulturelles/völkisches) Erbe*
Hispanic	a person whose first language is Spanish, esp. one who comes from a Latin American country	*Lateinamerikaner(in), Südamerikaner(in)*
to integrate sb.	to enable sb. to become accepted as a member of a social group	*jdn. miteinbeziehen, integrieren*
integration	the act of mixing previously-separated people	*Integration, Eingliederung*
(cultural) interaction	the act of communicating with sb. (from a different culture)	*gegenseitige (kulturelle) Einwirkung*

interracial	involving people of different races	*zwischen den verschiedenen Rassen*
to live on charity	to live on money/food/help that organizations or other people give/donate to sb.	*von Almosen leben*
multi-ethnic	involving or including several different races/ethnic groups/cultures	*Vielvölker-*
population	all the people who live in a particular area, city or country	*Bevölkerung*
scapegoat	a person who is blamed for sth. bad that sb. else has done or for failure;	*Sündenbock;* a fall guy; a whipping boy
segregation	the act/policy of separating people of different races	*Rassentrennung*

English word/phrase	Explanation in English	German equivalent and/or synonym(s)
Migration (from *Pathway, Einführungsphase*)		
to be at risk	to be in danger of sth. dangerous/unpleasant/harmful/happening	*gefährdet sein*
border/boundary	the line that divides two areas or countries	*Grenze*
to deport sb.	to force sb. to leave a country	*jdn. abschieben*
deportation	the act of forcing sb. to leave the country	*Abschiebung*

to emigrate	to leave your own country to go and live permanently in another country	*auswandern*
emigration	the act of leaving your own country	*Auswanderung*
to expel sb. [ɪk'spel]	to force sb. to leave a country	*jdn. ausweisen*
destination	a place that sb. is going or being sent to	*Bestimmungsort, Ziel*
famine ['fæmɪn]	a lack of food during a long period of time in an area/country	*Hungersnot*
for ethnic reasons	because of a person's race	*wegen der Volkszugehörigkeit/Abstammung*
homeland	the country where a person was born	*Heimat*
human rights	one of the basic rights that everyone is treated fairly and not in a cruel way, e. g. by their government	*Menschenrechte*
human trafficking	the act of buying and selling sb. illegally; to enslave sb.	*Menschenhandel*
to immigrate/ immigration	to come and live permanently in a country after leaving your own country	*einwandern; Einwanderung*
legal/illegal immigrant	a person who according to the law is (not) allowed to permanently live in a country after leaving his/her own country	*legaler/illegaler Einwanderer*
mass expulsion	the act of forcing sb. to leave a place	*Massenvertreibung*

migrant ['maɪgrənt]	a person who moves from one place to another, esp. to find work	*Gastarbeiter(in)/ Wanderarbeiter(in)*
migration	the movement of large numbers of people from one place to another	*(Ab-)Wanderung von Menschen*
out of economic necessity	for economic reasons	*wegen wirtschaftlicher Notwendigkeit/ Zwänge*
to persecute sb.	to act of treating sb. in an unfair and cruel way because of their race, gender, religion or beliefs	*jdn. verfolgen*
origin	a person's social and family background	*Herkunft, Abstammung;* ancesty; descent
persecution	the act of treating sb. in an unfair and cruel way because of their race, gender, religion or beliefs	*Verfolgung*
refugee ['refju'dʒiː]	a person who has been forced to leave their homeland because there is a war or for political, social or religious reasons	*Flüchtling; Asylant(in)*
transit	the process of being moved from one place to another	*Durchfahrt; Transport*

English word/phrase	Explanation in English	German equivalent and/or synonym(s)
Immigration policy (from *Pathway, Einführungsphase*)		
to address sth.	to take care of sth.	*etwas ansprechen/ thematisieren*

alien	a person who is not a citizen of the country in which they live or work	*Ausländer(in);* foreigner
asylum seeker [ə'saɪləm]	a person who has been forced to leave their own country to escape danger and who, after arriving in another country, asks to be allowed to stay there	*Asylant(in)*
to be a permanent resident	to live permanently at a place in a country/a city	*einen festen Wohnsitz haben*
border control	a system of controls to prevent illegal immigrants from entering a country, here: the border between the USA and Mexico	*Grenzkontrolle*
country of origin	country where a person was born	*Herkunftsland; Heimat*
illegal alien	an illegal immigrant	*illegale(r) Einwanderin/Einwanderer*
citizen	a person who has the legal right to belong to a particular country	*Staatsbürger*
citizenship	the legal right to belong to a particular country	*Staatsbürgerschaft*
economic migrant	a person who has left their homeland because the economic situation there is very bad	*Wirtschaftsflüchtling*

to exclude sb.	to prevent sb. from entering a place or taking part in sth.	*jdn. ausschließen*
exclusion	the act of preventing sb. from entering a place or taking part in sth.; banning sb. from sth.	*Ausschluss*
to flee (a country)	to escape from a country	*fliehen, flüchten;* to escape from
forcibly	in a way that involves the use of physical force	*unter Zwang*
immigration control	the place at a port, airport, etc. where the passports and other documents of the people coming into the country are checked	*Einwanderungskontrolle (z. B. Passkontrolle, Zoll etc.)*
to go through immigration	to pass the immigration control	*die Einwanderungskontrolle/Passkontrolle etc. durchlaufen*
immigration policy	the way a government deals with the immigration of people to its country	*Einwanderungspolitik*
influx [ˈɪnflʌks]	a large movement of people into a place from somewhere else	*Zustrom, Andrang, Zufluss*
legislation	the process of making and passing laws	*Gesetzgebung*
to pass legislation	to make a law official	*Inkrafttreten eines Gesetzes*
loyalty	the quality of being faithful in your support of sb.	*Treue, Loyalität*

naturalization [ˌnætʃəlaɪˈzeɪʃn]	the act of making sb. who was not born in a particular country a citizen of that country	*Einbürgerung, jdn. (offiziell) zum Staatsbürger eines Landes machen*
quota system	a system that allows only a limited number of people to immigrate	*Quotensystem*
restrictive	preventing people from doing what they want	*einschränkend*
to take an oath [əʊθ] **of allegiance** [əliːdʒəns]	a formal promise to support a country/party/leader/etc.	*den Treueeid schwören*

Democracy in the 21st Century – Views and Values

English word/phrase	Explanation in English	German equivalent and/or synonym(s)
	Democracy	
amendment	an addition to a law or document	*Gesetzesänderung; Zusatzartikel*
to appoint sb.	to choose sb. for a position	*jdn. berufen, jdn. ernennen*
ballot box	a box in which people put their ballots after voting	*Wahlurne*
ballot paper	the piece of paper on which sb. marks who they are voting for	*Wahlzettel*
to call an election	to arrange an election	*Wahlen ansetzen, eine Wahl ausschreiben*
to cast one's ballot/ vote	to vote in an election	*einen Stimmzettel/eine Stimme abgeben*
caucus ['kɔːkəs]	a meeting of the members of a political party to choose sb. to represent the party in an election	*(Fraktions-)Ausschuss, Parteiausschuss*
convention	a large meeting of the members of a political party	*Parteitag*
to declare sth. unconstitutional	to say officially or publicity that sth. is not allowed by the constitution	*etwas für nicht verfassungsmäßig erklären*
Electoral College	a group of people whose job is to choose a political leader	*Wahlmännergremium*

electorate	the people in a country who have the right to vote	*Wähler, Wählerschaft*
federal	related to the national government	*Bundes-*
inaugural address [ɪ'nɔːgjərəl]	the first speech a new leader gives when starting his work	*Amtsantrittsrede*
inauguration	the act of putting sb. into an official position with a ceremony	*Amtseinführung*
judiciary branch [dʒu'dɪʃəri brɑːntʃ]	all the courts that form part of the system of government	*Justiz, Justizwesen*
legislative branch [ledʒɪslətɪv brɑːntʃ]	the part of govern-ment concerned with making laws	*Legislative*
legislation	a law or a set of laws	*Gesetzgebung*
oath of office	a formal promise sb. takes before undertaking the duties of an office	*Amtseid*
to overrule a veto	to decide against a veto	*ein Veto überstimmen*
polling booth	a small separated place, where people vote	*Wahlkabine*
polling station	a building where people go to vote in an election	*Wahlbüro*
presidential nominee	sb. who has been formally suggested for President	*Präsidentschaftsanwär-ter*

primary (election)	an election in which people a particular area vote to choose a candidate for a important election	*Vorwahlen*
to run for President	to be a candidate in an election for President	*als Präsident(in) kandidieren*
separation of powers	the principle, that the political power of a government is separated	*Gewaltenteilung*
to serve a term	to spend a fixed or limited period of time in a job	*eine Amtszeit lang dienen*
to swear sb. in	to make sb. formally promise to do a job correctly, to be honest or loyal	*jdn. vereidigen*
system of checks and balances	the principle of government (in the US) by which the President, congress and the Supreme Court each have some control over the others	*System der Gewalten-kontrolle in einem Staat*
Vice-President [vaɪs ˈprezɪdənt]	the person who has the position immedi-ately below the president	*Vizepräsident*

English word/phrase	Explanation in English	German equivalent and/or synonym(s)
	Political systems	
administration	the government of a country at a particular time	*Regierung*

to amend (a bill) [ə'mend]	to correct or make changes to sth.	*(ein Gesetz) abändern, ergänzen*
to carry a decision	to accept a decision	*einen Entscheid annehmen/mittragen*
Chancellor of the Exchequer	(in Britain) the government minister who is responsible for financial affairs	*Finanzminister(in)*
consent [kən'sent]	agreement	*Einvernehmen, Einverständnis*
constituency [kən'stɪtjuənsi]	a district that elects its own representative to parliament	*Wahlbezirk*
(constitutional) monarchy	a country with a king or queen whose power is controlled by a set of laws and basic principles	*(konstitutionelle) Monarchie*
to dissolve (parliament)	to officially end (parliament)	*auflösen*
domestic policy	of or inside a particular country; not foreign or international	*Innenpolitik*
to draw up a bill	to design a law	*ein Gesetz entwerfen*
to be eligible ['elɪdʒəbl] **to vote**	to be legally allowed to vote	*wahlberechtigt sein*
first-past-the-post system	a voting system in which only the person who gets the most votes is elected	*Mehrheitswahlrecht*
foreign policy	policy dealing with or involving other countries	*Außenpolitik*

Foreign Secretary	the British politician who is in charge of the Foreign Office and the political relationship with other countries	*Außenminister(in)*
to have a say in sth.	the right to influence sth. by giving your opinion before a decision is made	*ein Mitspracherecht haben*
hereditary peer	sb. who is holding a title that is hereditary	*Mitglied des Oberhauses mit erblichem Titel*
Home Secretary	the British government minister in charge of the Home Office	*Innenminister(in)*
House of Commons	the part of the British parliament whose members are elected by the people	*Unterhaus*
House of Lords	the part of the British parliament whose members are not elected but have positions because of their rank or title	*Oberhaus*
legislative ['ledʒɪslətɪv] **period**	the period of time during which sb. does the job they were elected for	*Legislaturperiode*
life peer	sb. who is given the honour of a title such as 'Lord' and a place in the House of Lords as a reward for the good things they have done for the country	*Mitglied des Oberhauses auf Lebenszeit*

Lord Chancellor	the most important official in the legal system of England and Wales	*Präsident(in) des Oberhauses und Justizminister(in)*
majority vote	a voting system in which only the person who gets the most votes is elected	*Mehrheitswahlrecht*
peer	member of the House of Lords	*Mitglied des Oberhauses*
policy	a plan of action agreed of chosen by a political party	*eine bestimmte Politik*
politics	the activities of the government, members of law-making organizations or people who try to influence the way a country is governed	*Politik im Allgemeinen*
to preside over sth.	to lead or be in charge of a formal meeting, ceremony, etc.	*den Amtsvorsitz haben*
proportional representation	a political system in which parties are represented in parliament according to the number of people who voted for them	*Verhältniswahlrecht*
to reject a bill	to refuse to accept or not to accept a bill	*einen Gesetzesentwurf ablehnen*
Speaker	the title of the person whose job is to control the discussions in a parliament	*Vorsitzender des Unterhauses*

to stand down	to leave a job or position	*abtreten;* to step down
to toe [təʊ] **the party line**	to support the official opinion of a political party	*sich nach der Parteilinie richten*
universal suffrage ['sʌfrɪdʒ]	the right of all the people in the country to vote	*allgemeines Wahlrecht*
to veto ['viːtəʊ] **a bill/a law**	to refuse to accept a bill/a law	*ein(en) Gesetz/-esentwurf ablehnen*

English word/phrase	Explanation in English	German equivalent and/or synonym(s)
	The United Nations	
to adopt (a charter)	to formally approve sth., esp. by voting	*eine Charta verabschieden*
annual session	a session, which is happening or done every year	*jährliche Sitzung*
collective military action	a military action, that is done or shared by every members of a group	*gemeinsame militärische Aktion*
to be committed to doing sth.	to say that sb. will definitely do sth.	*sich verpflichten, etwas zu tun*
to be determined [dɪ'tɜːmɪnd]	having a strong desire to do sth., so that you will not let anyone prevent you	*sich verpflichtet fühlen*
diplomacy [dɪ'pləʊməsi]	the job or activity of managing the relationships between countries	*Diplomatie*
to enforce sth.	to make sth. happen or force sb. to do sth.	*etw. durchsetzen;* to put sth. through

General Assembly	the group that represents all of the countries which belong to the United Nations	*Vollversammlung*
to impose sanctions	to start using official orders or laws as a way of forcing e. g. a leader of another country to make political changes	*Sanktionen verhängen*
to interfere with sth.	to get involved in and try to influence a situation	*sich in etwas einmischen*
to lay out an agenda	to present an agenda clearly and carefully	*ein Programm aufstellen/darlegen*
to maintain peace	to make peace continue	*Frieden aufrechterhalten/erhalten*
to mediate between	to try to end a disagreement between two or more people or groups by talking to them	*vermitteln*
to meet sb.'s needs	to do or satisfy what is needed or what sb. asks for	*jds. Bedürfnisse befriedigen*
objective	sth. that you are trying hard to achieve	*Ziel, Zielsetzung;* aim
permanent representatives	the head of a diplomatic mission to one of various international organisations, e. g. the United Nations	*ständige Vertreter*
to provide sth.	to give sth. to sb. or make it available for them to use	*etwas bereitstellen*

rotating (non-permanent) member	sb. who is a member just for a particular time	*wechselndes Mitglied*
trade embargo	trade boycott	*Handelsembargo, Handelssperre*
tribunal [traɪˈbjuːnl]	a type of court that is given official authority to deal with a problem	*Tribunal, Gericht*

Africa: The Dark Continent – A Beacon of Hope?

English word/phrase	Explanation in English	German equivalent and/or synonym(s)
	Historical Development	
ancient ['eɪnʃənt]	very old	*sehr alt*
to come into existence	to start being	*entstehen*
collapse of sth.	the end of failure of sth.	*Zerfall, Zusammenbruch*
(political) crisis (pl. crises)	a time of great anger, difficulty or confusion when (political) problems must be solved or important decisions must be made	*(politische) Krise*
to defeat sb./sth.	to win a victory over sb. in a war, fight, etc.	*besiegen, bezwingen*
defeat of sb./sth.	the act of winning a victory over sb./sth.	*Besiegung, Sieg*
formation of sth.	creation of sth.	*Anordnung, Entstehung*
to found sth.	to build or establish sth.	*etw. errichten*
foundation of sth.	the establishment of sth.	*Gründung, Grundlage*
to invade	to enter a country/an area using military force in order to control it	*einmarschieren*
to join (a union)	to become a member of a group/an organization	*sich in etwas einreihen, sich angliedern*

(historical) landmark	one of the most important events/ changes or discoveries	*(historischer) Meilenstein, Wendepunkt*
modernity [mə'dɜːnəti]	the condition of being new modern	*Modernität*
occupation of sth.	the act of moving into a country, town, etc. and taking control of it using military force	*Belagerung*
to occupy	to enter a place in a large group and take control of it, especially by military force	*belagern*
phenomenon [fə'nɒmɪnən]	a fact or an event in nature or society, especially one that is not fully understood	*Erscheinung, Phänomen*
(leading) power	a country that is strong and important and can influence events, or that has a lot of military strength	*Führungsmacht, Weltmacht*
prehistory	the time in history before everything was written down	*Vorzeit, Vorgeschichte*
to rebel [rɪ'bel]	to fight against or refuse to obey an authority, e.g. a government	*rebellieren, auflehnen*
rebellion [rɪ'beljən]	an attempt by some of the people in a country to change their government	*Aufstand, Rebellion*
revolt [rɪ'vəʊlt]	a protest against authority, especially that of a government, often involving violence	*Revolte, Aufstand*

to revolt against sb./ sth.	to take violent action against the people in power	*revoltieren, aufbegehren*
tribal ['traɪbl]	connected with a tribe or tribes	*Stammes-*
tribe	a group of people of the same race, and with the same customs, language, religion, etc. living in a particular area	*(Volks-) Stamm*

English word/phrase	Explanation in English	German equivalent and/or synonym(s)
Colonization		
the acquisition of colonies	the act of getting land	*Beschaffung, Übernahme v. Kolonien*
to civilize sb.	to improve a society so that it is more organized and developed	*zivilisieren*
to claim a territory	to demand or ask for territory because you believe it is your legal right	*Territorium beanspruchen*
(colonial) policy	a way of doing sth. that has been officially agreed upon and chosen by a political party or government	*(Kolonial-) Politik*
to colonize	to establish political control over another country, and send your citizens there to settle	*kolonialisieren*

colonization [ˌkɒlənaɪˈzeɪʃn]	the act of establishing political control over another country and sending your citizens there to settle	*Kolonialisierung*
colonist	sb. who settles in a new colony	*Kolonist*
to gain control over sb.	to obtain control over sb.	*Kontrolle über jdn. erlangen*
to conquer [ˈkɒŋkə(r)]	to gain control of a country by fighting	*erobern*
conqueror	a person (often part of an army) who fights to gain control of a country	*Eroberer*
conquest	the act of gaining control of a country	*Eroberung*
to decolonize sb.	to make a former colony politically independent	*in die Unabhängigkeit entlassen, entkolonisieren*
discovery	the act of discovering sth.	*das Entdecken*
to divide sth. up	to separate sth. into parts and share them between people	*aufteilen*
to explore	to travel to an area in order to find out what it is like/what is there	*erkunden, auskundschaften*
exploration	the act of travelling through a place in order to find out about it or find resources, etc.	*Erforschung, Erkundung*
to invade	to enter a country using military force in order to take control of it	*einmarschieren, einfallen*

invasion [ɪn'veɪʒn]	the act of invading a country	*Invasion, Einmarsch*
mother country	the country where you or your family where born and which you feel a strong emotional connection with	*Heimatland*
native	sb. who was born in a particular country or area	*Ureinwohner*
negotiations	diplomatic talks to reach an agreement	*Verhandlungen*
post-colonial	after colonialism	*postcolonial*

English word/phrase	Explanation in English	German equivalent and/or synonym(s)
Trade		
to benefit from sth.	to profit from sth.	*von etw. profitieren*
benefit	advantage	*Vorteil, Nutzen*
commerce	trade	*Handel*
economic power	the fact of having a lot of influence because of being able to produce, buy, or sell a lot	*Wirtschaftskraft*
(economic) supremacy [suː'preməsi]	a position in which you have more power, authority or status than anyone else	*Übermacht, Überlegenheit*
industrialized country	a country which is having many industries	*Industriestaat/-nation*
to manufacture sth.	to produce sth.	*herstellen, produzieren*
to provide sth.	to make sth. available	*zur Verfügung stellen*

raw [rɔː] **materials**	natural substances that are used in manufacturing goods	*Rohstoffe, Rohmaterial*
resources [rɪ'sɔːsəz]	soil, minerals, forests, water and energy sources	*Ressourcen*
to run sth. for profit	to do sth. because you want to make money with it	*etw. für Profit/aus Profitgründen tun*
secure markets	safe markets	*sichere Märkte*
to trade with	to buy and sell goods as your business	*handeln mit*
trading post/trading station	a place where people can buy and exchange goods in a country	*Handelsstation, Handelsposten*
trading company	a business that buys and sells goods, esp. internationally	*Handelsgesellschaft*
transatlantic trade	trade/business involving countries on both sides of the Atlantic	*transatlantischer Handel*
transportation network	a system of roads/channels/railroads to transport goods	*Verkehrsnetz, Transportnetzwerk*
triangular [traɪ'æŋgjələ(r)] **trade**	trade involving three continents: Europe, Africa and America	*Dreieckshandel*
wealth	a large amount of money, property or valuable possessions that a person or a country owns	*Reichtum*

Society – Living Together in a Small World

English word/phrase	Explanation in English	German equivalent and/or synonym(s)
	Urbanization	
to accommodate	to provide sb. with a room or place to sleep or live	*jdm. unterbringen/ beherbergen*
accommodation	a place to live, work or stay	*Unterkunft*
campus	the buildings of a university or college and the land around them	*Campus (Universität)*
communal	shared by or for the use of a number of people, esp. people who live together	*gemeinsam*
decentralization [ˌdiːˌsentrəlaɪˈzeɪʃn]	the act of moving parts of a government, organization, etc. from a central place to several different smaller ones	*Dezentralisierung*
degradation	the process of sth. being damaged or made worse	*Degradierung, Abbau*
exclusion	the act of not being included	*Ausschluss*
facade [fəˈsɑːd]	the front of a building	*Fassade*
gated community	a group of houses surrounded by a wall or fence, with an entrance that is guarded	*bewachtes Wohnviertel*

(historical/cultural) heritage	the traditional beliefs, values, customs, etc. of a familiy, country, or society	*(historisches/ kulturelles) Erbe*
to house sb.	to provide a place for sb. to live	*jdn. unterbringen/ beherbergen*
inclusion	the act of including sb.	*Einschluss*
intergenerational	between or involving people from different age groups	*generationsübergrei- fend*
metropolitan	connected with a large or capital city	*hauptstädtisch/ großstädtisch*
municipal	connected to a city	*städtisch, Stadt-, kommunal*
occupation *(fml.)*	the act of living in a building/area, etc.	*Besitz, Bewohnen*
to occupy	to live or stay in a place	*bewohnen;* to inhabit
pedestrian zone	a shopping area in the centre of a town where cars, trucks, etc. cannot go	*Fußgängerzone*
public transport	buses, trains, etc. that are available for everyone to use	*öffentliche Verkehrsmit- tel*
recreation grounds/ areas	an area of public land used by the public for sports and games	*Freizeitgelände*
resident	sb. who lives in a particular place or who has their home there	*Bewohner*
residential (area)	a residential area consists of private houses rather than offices or factories	*Wohngegend*

skyscraper	a very tall modern city building	*Wolkenkratzer*
(social) equity ['ekwəti]	fairness	*(soziale) Gerechtigkeit*
social networks	websites or services on the Internet which are used to communicate with people who share your interests	*soziale Netzwerke (z.B. facebook)*
suburban	in or connected with an area where people live that is outside the centre of a city	*Vorstadt-*
sustainability-oriented	involving the use of natural products and energy, causing little or no damage to the environment and therefore able to continue for a long time	*nachhaltig*
urban/urbanization	relating to towns and cities/the process by which more and more people live and work in towns and cities rather than in the countryside	*städtisch/Verstädterung*

English word/phrase	Explanation in English	German equivalent and/or synonym(s)
Society/values		
accessible [ək'sesəbl]	able to be reached	*verfügbar, zugänglich*
to have access to sth.	to have the opportunity or right to use sth.	*Zugang zu etwas haben*
alienation	the feeling of not being part of a group	*Fremdheit*

to ban sb./sth.	to prohibit or forbid sth.	*etwas verbieten*
civic duties	sth. you have to do or that you are responsible for because you are a citizen of a country or community	*staatsbürgerliche Pflichten*
community-building	to encourage the feeling of sharing things or belonging to a group in the place where you live	*gemeinschaftsbildend*
community interests	civil duty	*Anziehungskraft einer Gemeinde*
discriminatory [dɪ'skrɪmɪnətəri]	treating sb. or a group of people worse than others in an unfair way	*diskriminierend*
discrimination of sb.	the practice of treating sb. or a particular group in society less fairly than others	*Diskriminierung von jdm.*
diversity [daɪ'vɜːsəti]	a range of different people, things or ideas	*Vielfalt*
freedom of expression	the freedom to say or write what you think or feel	*Freiheit der Meinungsäußerung*
fundamentalism ['fʌndə'mentəlɪzəm]	the practice of following very strictly the basic rules of any religion	*Fundamentalismus*
(gender) repression	the act of using force to control a group of people and restrict their freedom	*(Geschlechter-) Unterdrückung*

internal (social) stability	the maintenance, constancy and reliability of social systems, e.g. patterns of relationships like family, work, business, etc.	*innere (soziale) Stabilität*
Islamophobic	having hatred or fear of Muslims	*Anti-Islamismus*
limitation	restriction	*Begrenzung, Einschränkung*
to meet sb.'s (basic) needs	to do or satisfy what is needed or sb. asks for	*jds. Grundbedürfnisse erfüllen*
multiculturalism	the practice of giving importance to all cultures in a society	*Multikulturalismus*
opinionated	having very strong opinions that you are not willing to change	*eigensinnig, voreingenommen*
pluralism	the existence of many different groups of people in one society	*Pluralismus*
prejudice	an unreasonable dislike and distrust of people who are different from you in some way	*Vorurteil*
to be prejudiced	having an unreasonable dislike of or preference for sb./sth.	*voreingenommen sein*
religious community	a group of people who have the same religion	*religiöse Gemeinschaft*
respect for sb./sth.	a feeling of admiration for sb./sth. because of their good qualities or achievements	*Respekt vor jdm./etw.*

to respect sb./sth.	to have a very good opinion of sb./sth.	*jdn./etw. respektieren*
to stand out	to be easily seen; to be noticeable	*auffallen*
to undermine sth.	to make sth., esp. sb.'s confidence or authority, gradually weaker	*etwas untergraben*

English word/phrase	Explanation in English	German equivalent and/or synonym(s)
Megacities		
to accelerate	to make sth. happen faster or sooner	*beschleunigen*
acceleration	an increase in how fast sth. happens	*Beschleunigung*
air pollution	the process of making air dirty; the state of being dirty	*Luftverschmutzung*
availability of sth.	the fact that sth. can be bought, used or reached	*Verfügbarkeit*
contamination	the act of making a substance or place dirty	*Verunreinigung, Belastung*
corrugated iron shacks	a very small and simple building made from pieces of corrugated metal or other materials	*Wellblechhütten*
decline	reduction in size or number	*Abnahme*
densely populated	containing a lot of people living with little space between them	*dicht bevölkert*

deprivation [ˌdeprɪˈveɪʃn]	the fact of not having sth. that you need	*Verlust, Entzug*
deterioration [dɪˈtɪərɪəˈreɪʃn]	the act of becoming worse	*Verfall, Verschlechte-rung*
diversity [daɪˈvɜːsəti]	a range of many people or things that are very different from each other	*Vielfalt, Mannigfaltig-keit*
economic concentra-tion	a large amount of economics in a particular place	*Wirtschaftskonzentra-tion*
expansion of city boundaries	the process by which a city increases in size	*Ausweitung von Stadtgrenzen*
food scarcity	a situation in which there is not enough food	*Lebensmittelmangel*
habitat loss	the loss of places where a particular plant or animal lives	*Verlust des Lebensrau-mes*
housing	the houses, flats, apartments, etc. that people live in	*Unterkunft, Unterbrin-gung*
increase	growth	*Wachstum*
inefficient [ˌɪnɪˈfɪʃnt]	not doing a job well and making poor use of time, energy, etc.	*ineffizient, unwirt-schaftlich*
(massive) infrastruc-ture	the basis system and services that are necessary for a country or an organization to run smoothly	*(starke) Infrastruktur*
megacity	a city over 10 million inhabitants	*Millionenstadt, Metropole*

population density	the degree to which an area is filled with people	*Bevölkerungsdichte*
shelter	a place to live or stay	*Unterkunft, Unterschlupf*
slum dweller	sb. who lives in a slum	*Slumbewohner*
social unrest	a political situation in which people are angry and likely to protest or fight	*soziale Unruhe(n)*
(to) sprawl	an act of spreading to cover a large area in an untidy way	*sich ausbreiten, wuchern*

Economy, Energy, Efficiency – The World Going Global

English word/phrase	Explanation in English	German equivalent and/or synonym(s)
	Globalisation	
capital market	financial market	*Finanzmarkt, Kapitalmarkt*
communication technology	the use of computers and other electronic equipment etc.	*Informations-/ Kommunikationstechnik*
cultural imperialism	the imposing of a foreign culture on sb.	*kultureller Imperialismus*
domestic demand	the amount of money that is spent on goods and services by the people, companies, and government within a particular country	*inländische Nachfrage*
domestic labour	the working situation within a particular country	*inländischer Arbeitsmarkt*
economic tie	economic connection to sb.	*Wirtschaftsverbindung*
entrepreneurship [ˌɒntrəprəˈnɜː(r)ʃɪp]	running one's own business	*Unternehmertum*
exploitation	an unfair treatment used to show disapproval	*Ausbeutung*
to exploit	to treat sb. unfairly by asking them things to do for you, but giving them very little in return	*ausbeuten*
to generate capital	to earn money	*Kapital erzeugen (Geld verdienen)*

to hold a patent	to have a special document that says that no one else is allowed to copy a product except for the inventor	*Patent auf etw. haben*
to increase purchasing power	to raise people's ability to buy goods	*die Kaufkraft erhöhen*
infrastructure	the basic systems and services, such as transport or power supplies that a country or organization uses in order to work effectively	*Infrastruktur*
interdependency	a situation in which people or things depend on each other	*Korrelation, gegenseitige Abhängigkeit*
international trade	trade between different countries	*internationaler Handel*
to be internationalized	to make sth. become international	*internationalisiert sein*
to invest in sb./sth.	to spend money on sth. in order to gain sth. back	*in etw./jdn. investieren*
investment in	sth. that you buy or do because it will be useful later	*Investition in*
labour standards	the working conditions	*Arbeitsstandard*
liberalization of sth.	the act of making sth. less strict	*Liberalisierung von etw.*
logistics	the practical organization of sth.	*Logistik*
microcredit ['mɒɪkrəʊˌkredɪt]	a small credit	*Mikrokredit, Kleinkredit*

microloan	a very small credit given to sb.	*Mikrokredit, Kleinkredit*
migration [maɪ'greɪʃn]	when large numbers of people go to live in another area or country esp. in order to find work	*Migration (Wanderung)*
migrant worker	sb. who goes to live in another country in order to find work there	*Wanderarbeiter*
multinationals	internationally cooperating companies	*multinationale Konzerne*
output	the amount of sth. that a company produces	*Produktion, Leistung*
outsourcing of work	the act of arranging for sb. outside the company to do work for that company	*Fremdarbeit*
to outsource	to arrange for sb. outside the company to do a job, e. g. in another country	*ausgliedern*
to promote international trade	to do sth. in order to increase the international trade	*internationalen Handel fördern*
protective tariff	a tax intended to increase prices of imports and protect a country's industries from foreign competition	*Schutzzoll*
protectionism	when a government tries to help industries in its own country by taxing or restricting goods from other countries	*Protektionismus, Schutzpolitik*

to raise living-standards	to level up the comfort and the amount of money that people have	*Lebensstandards erhöhen*
standardized	to make all the things of one particular type the same alike	*standardisiert*
sweatshop ['swet ʃɒp]	a small factory where workers are paid very little and work many hours in very bad conditions	*Ausbeuterbetrieb*
technological innovation	a new technological idea, method or invention	*technologische/r Innovation/Fortschritt*
trade negotiation	discussion about economic affairs in order to reach an agreement	*Wirtschafts-verhandlung(en)*
uniformity	the quality of being or looking the same as all members of a group	*Einheitlichkeit;* standardization
unskilled (worker)	not been trained for a particular type of job	*ungelernter Arbeiter*

English word/phrase	Explanation in English	German equivalent and/or synonym(s)
Consumerism/consumption		
acquisition of sth.	the act of buying sth.	*Anschaffung, Erwerb*
availability	**the fact that sb. is free to work, be contacted, etc., or whether or how much they can**	*Verfügbarkeit*
to be available to sb.	able to be reached by sb.	*erhältlich, verfügbar für jdn. sein*

to cash a paycheck	to exchange a cheque for the amount of money it is worth	*einen Gehaltsscheck einlösen*
consumer	sb. who buys and uses products and services	*Konsument*
customer	sb. who buys goods or services from a shop, company etc.	*Kunde*
discount shopping	to go shopping at a store that sells goods cheaply	*im Discount einkaufen*
to display sth.	to present sth.	*etw. anzeigen*
distribution of sth.	the act of giving or delivering things to a large group of people	*Verteilung*
efficiency [ɪˈfɪʃnsi]	the quality of doing sth. well without wasting money or time	*Effizienz, Leistungsfähigkeit*
industrialized mass production	when products are made in large numbers by industrial machines so they can be sold cheaply	*industrialisierte Massenproduktion*
to instil a desire	to put the idea in sb.'s mind, that they desire sth.	*jdm. eine Begierde einflößen*
Internet retailer	Internet shop	*Internethändler*
to line the shelves	to offer sth. for sale in large amounts	*den Absatz steigern*
mounting consumer debt	strongly rising consumer debt	*steigende Konsumverschuldung*
online shopping portal	a website where you can buy things by choosing them online	*Online-Einkaufsportal*

price spiral [spaɪrəl]	a continual rise in prices	*Preisspirale*
purchasing power	the amount of money a person or group has available to spent	*Kaufkraft*
shipping	the delivery of goods	*Lieferung*
status symbol	sth. that you have or own that shows high social rank or position	*Statussymbol*
range of products	selection of products	*Produktumfang*
retailer	a person or store that sells goods	*Händler, Einzelhändler*
retail store	store that sells goods to the public	*Einzelhandelsgeschäft*
supermarket chain	a large number of supermarkets from the same company in different places	*Supermarktkette*

English word/phrase	Explanation in English	German equivalent and/or synonym(s)
	Ecology/energy	
agriculture	the practice of farming	*Landwirtschaft*
biodegradable [ˌbaɪəʊdɪˈgreɪdəbl]	sth. changed naturally by bacteria into substances that do not harm the environment	*biologisch abbaubar*
carbon emission	carbon dioxide that planes, cars, factories, etc. produce, which is harmful to the environment	*Kohlenstoffausstoß*
climate change	a permanent change in weather conditions	*Klimawandel*

crops	plants that are grown by farmers and used as food	*Ernten*
deforestation	the cutting or burning down of all the trees in an area	*Waldrodung*
to dump sth.	to throw sth. away	*etw. wegschmeißen*
exploitation	here: the use of land, oil, minerals	*Ausbeutung*
fragility of sth.	easily broken or damaged	*Zerbrechlichkeit*
fossil fuel	fuel such as coal and oil, which were formed underground from plant and animal remains millions of years ago	*fossiler Brennstoff*
greenhouse effect	the gradual warming of the air surrounding the earth as a result of heat being trapped by pollution	*Treibhauseffekt*
habitat	natural home of a plant or animal	*Lebensraum*
to have an impact on sth.	to influence sth.	*etw. beeinflussen*
heatwave	a period of unusually hot weather	*Hitzewelle*
the incineration of trash	the act of burning trash in a facility	*Müllverbrennung*
to pose a threat for/to sb.	sb. or sth. that is regarded as a possible danger	*für jdn. eine Bedrohung darstellen*

renewable energies	types of energy such as wind power or solar equipment that can be replaced as quickly as they are used	*erneuerbare Energien*
sustainability	able to continue for a long time without causing damage to the environment	*Nachhaltigkeit*
techniques of cultivation	techniques of using land	*Anbautechniken*
waste disposal	garbage disposal	*Müllentsorgung*
water supply	the water that is provided and treated for a particular area	*Wasserversorgung*

English word/phrase	Explanation in English	German equivalent and/or synonym(s)
Environment (from *Pathway, Einführungsphase*)		
airborne	in the air	*in der Luft befindlich*
to avert sth. [ə'vɛːt]	to prevent sth. from happening	*etwas abwenden, verhindern*
to become extinct	to no longer exist, to cease to exist	*aussterben*
biodegradable [ˌbaɪəʊdɪgreɪdəbl]	changing a substance into a harmless natural state by using bacteria	*kompostierbar*
crude oil	oil that is in its natural condition before it made pure or separated into different products	*Rohöl*
to decompose	to rot	*verrotten, kompostie-ren*

deforestation	cutting or burning down trees	*Abholzung/Rodung von Wald*
to dispose of sth.	to get rid of sth.	*sich einer Sache entledigen*
environmentally-friendly	not harmful to the environment	*umweltfreundlich*
environmental safe-guard	institution that helps protect the environment from damage	*Umweltschutzeinrichtung*
fossil fuel	fuel such as coal or oil, formed over millions of years from the remains of animals or plants	*fossilie Brennstoffe (z. B. Öl, Kohle)*
greenhouse effect	the problem of the gradual rise in temperature in the air surrounding the earth	*globale Erderwärmung*, a global warming
habitat	a natural home of a plant or animal	*Lebensraum*
to incinerate	to burn sth.	*etwas verbrennen*
to intensify sth.	to heighten	*etwas verstärken, intensivieren*
insulation	material used to insulate sth., esp. a building (e. g. glass fibre insulation)	*Isolation (Gebäude)*
(ir-)reversible	sth. that can(not) be changed back	*(nicht) umkehrbar*
organic farming	farming without using chemicals	*organische Landwirtschaft*
ozone layer	a layer of gases in the sky that prevents harmful radiation from the sun reaching the earth	*Ozonschicht*

to play a vital role in sth.	to be very important	*eine wesentliche Rolle spielen*
power station	large plant where electricity is produced	*Kraftwerk*
precipitation	rain, snow, etc. that falls	*Niederschlag*
to prevent sb./sth. from doing sth.	to stop sb. from achieving an aim/sth. from happening	*verhindern, dass jmd. etwas tut/etwas geschieht*
raw material	material before being processed	*Rohstoff*
to reduce sth.	to decrease or become sth. smaller	*verringern, reduzieren*
reduction	the process of making sth. decrease or become smaller	*Reduzierung, Verkleinerung*
reforestation	planting new trees/ forests	*Wiederaufforstung*
solar radiation	energy in the form of heat that is sent out from the sun	*Sonneneinstrahlung*
source	the origin of sth.	*Quelle*
to supply the demand for sth.	to produce or deliver enough of sth.	*den Bedarf decken*
unleaded [ˌʌnˈledɪd] **petrol**	unleaded petrol does not contain any lead	*bleifreies Benzin*
vapour	a mass of very small drops of liquid which float in the air	*Dampf*
water supply	the amount of water that is available to be used	*Wasserversorgung*

English word/phrase	Explanation in English	German equivalent and/or synonym(s)
Pollution (from *Pathway, Einführungsphase*)		
acidic content	the amount of acid that sth. contains	*Säuregehalt*
carbon dioxide ['kɒːbən daɪ'ksaɪd]	the gas produced when animals breathe out, when carbon is burned in air or when animals or vegetable substances decay	*Kohlendioxid*
to contaminate	to pollute	*verschmutzen*
to corrode sth.	to destroy sth. by chemical action	*korrodieren, zerstören*
depletion [dɪ'pliːʃn] **(of the ozone layer)**	reduction of ...	*Verringerung von ...*
detergent	substance that helps remove dirt	*Reinigungsmittel*
to discharge sth.	to send out a substance	*etwas ablassen*
to dump	to get rid of sth.	*wegwerfen*
dyestuffs	chemicals that are used to dye or colour e.g. textiles	*Färbemittel*
emission	a gas or substance that is sent into the air	*Schadstoffausstoß*
excess packaging	more packaging than necessary/usual/legal	*unnütze/überflüssige Verpackung*
to exploit sb.	here: to develop and use minerals, forests, oils, etc. for business or industry	*ausnutzen, ausbeuten*
to expose sth./sb. to sth.	to put sb./sth. in a situation where they are not protected from sth. dangerous	*sich etwas (einer Gefahr) aussetzen*

fertilizer	a substance that is put on the soil to make plants grow	*Dünger*
fumes	smoke	*Abgase*
to have an adverse effect on sth.	to have a negative/ unpleasant effect	*eine schädliche Wirkung haben*
to harm	to hurt/to injure	*verletzen, schaden*
intensive farming	farming practised on small areas of land with high inputs (of fertilizers, etc.)	*intensive Landwirtschaft*
irrigation	the act of supplying land or crops with water	*künstliche Bewässerung*
landfill	a place where waste is buried under the ground	*Mülldeponie*
lead [led]	a soft grey heavy metal that melts easily and is poisonous	*Blei*
to leak oil	to lose oil	*Öl verlieren/lecken*
living conditions	the conditions under which people live, e.g. income, housing, etc.	*Lebensbedingungen*
mercury	a heavy silver-white poisonous metal	*Quecksilber*
oil spill	oil, that accidently flows into the ocean, e.g. after an explosion and contaminates the water	*Ölpest*
pesticide ['pestɪsaɪd]	a chemical substance used to kill insects or small animals that destroy crops	*Schädlingsbekämpfungsmittel*

pollutant	a substance that makes sth. dirty or unsafe to use	*Schadstoff*
pollution	the process of making air/water dirty	*Verschmutzung*
propellant	gas which is used in an aerosol to spray out a liquid	*Treibmittel*
refrigerant	a substance that is used in fridges and freezes to cool sth.	*Kühlmittel*
residues *(pl.)* ['rezɪdjuːs]	a substance that remains on a surface and cannot be removed easily	*Rückstände*
sewage ['suːɪdʒ] **treatment plant**	a place where sewage is treated to stop it being harmful	*Kläranlage*
to stunt growth	to stop/reduce growth	*das Wachstum hemmen*
substance	a particular type of solid, liquid or gas	*Substanz*
sulphuric ['sʌlfərɪk] **acid**	a powerful acid	*Schwefelsäure*
sulphur dioxide	a poisonous gas that is a cause of our pollution in industrial areas	*Schwefeldioxid*
waste	garbage, litter	*Müll*
to waste	to use more of sth. than is necessary	*verschwenden*

English word/phrase	Explanation in English	German equivalent and/or synonym(s)
Recycling (from *Pathway, Einführungsphase*)		
to address sth.	to take care of sth./to deal with a situation	*sich um etw. kümmern/etw. in Angriff nehmen*
to contribute to sth.	to be one of the causes of sth.	*zu etwas beitragen*
to cope with a problem	to manage or deal with a problem	*mit einem Problem umgehen/es lösen*
to donate	to give sth., esp. money to a person or an organization in order to help them	*spenden*
ecosystem	a natural unit consisting of all plants, animals and microorganisms in an area functioning together	*Ökosystem*
energy-efficient	doing sth. without wasting energy	*energiesparend*
geothermal energy	energy relating to or coming from the heat inside the earth	*Erdwärme*
metal scrap	metal that is no longer used for the purpose it was made for but can be used again in another way	*Metallschrott*
mixed (loads of) litter	waste of different materials, e.g. papers, plastic, metal, etc.	*unsortierter Müll*
paper processing	the rense of old paper	*Altpapierverwertung*
to recover sth.	to get sth. that was lost	*etwas zurückgewinnen*

to recycle waste	to pass a substance through a system that enables all or part of that substance to be reused	*Müll/Abfall wiederverwerten*
renewable	renewable energy replaces itself naturally	*erneuerbar*
to reprocess sth.	to recycle sth.	*etw. wiederverwerten*
returnable	able to be taken back to a store in order to be used again	*umtauschbar*
to reuse	to use sth. again	*wiederverwerten*
rubble	broken stones or bricks from a destroyed or damaged building	*Geröll*
sewage treatment plant	a place where sewage is treated to stop it being harmful	*Kläranlage*
solar energy	light and heat of the sun that is used to produce energy	*Sonnenenergie*
sort line	a system of making waste moving past a line of workers who sort out recyclable materials	*Müllsortierungsanlage (Fließband)*
to sort rubbish	to separate different waste	*Müll trennen*
sustainable	involving the use of natural products that do not harm the environment	*nachhaltig*

English word/phrase	Explanation in English	German equivalent and/or synonym(s)
Work (from *Pathway, Einführungsphase*)		
to apply for (a job)	to make a formal request for sth.	*sich für eine Stelle bewerben*
basic requirement	a fundamental quality that sb./sth. has to have to meet a certain standard/sb.'s expectations	*Grundvoraussetzung*
blind application	enquiry about the possibility of a job even though one hasn't been advertised	*sich auf eine (nicht ausgeschriebene) Stelle bewerben*
competitive	trying hard to be better than others	*ehrgeizig;* ambitious
computer literacy	ability to handle a computer	*mit einem Computer umgehen können*
corporate image	the image of a company that all its members should display to the public	*Unternehmensphilosophie, das Ansehen eines Unternehmens;* the reputation of a company
CV [ˌsiːˌviː] **(Curriculum Vitae)** *(BE)*	a short written document that lists sb.'s education and previous jobs	*Lebenslauf*
to employ sb.	to give sb. a job	*jdn. anstellen/ beschäftigen*
employee	a person who is paid to work for sb.	*Angestellte(r)*
employment legislation	the laws connected with work, workers, etc.	*Arbeitsrecht*

to go freelance	to earn money by selling your work to many different companies/organizations	*selbstständig/ freiberuflich tätig sein*
to gain work experience	the experience you have had working in a particular job	*ein Praktikum machen*
job advert	an advertisement published by a company to find new employees	*Stellenanzeige*
job interview	interview held by a company to find out about a potential new employee's qualifications and motivation	*Vorstellungsgespräch*
job market	the people looking for work and the number of jobs that are available	*Arbeitsmarkt*
letter of application	letter that sb. writes to a company to apply for a job	*Bewerbungsschreiben*
qualification(s)	a skill or type of experience that you need for a particular job	*Qualifikation, Fähigkeit(en)*
to recruit sb./ recruitment	to find new people to join a company	*jdn. anwerben/ einstellen; Anwerbung/ Einstellung*
to renew a contract	to extend a contract	*einen Arbeitsvertrag erneuern/verlängern*
résumé *(US)* ['rezjumeɪ]	a short written document that lists your education and previous jobs	*Lebenslauf*

to retrain	to learn a new type of work/a new skill	*umschulen*
(un)skilled	(not) having special training/qualifications	*(un-)gelernt, (un-) ausgebildet*
semi-skilled	having some special training/qualifications but less than skilled people	*angelernt (d. h. mit Berufskenntnissen, aber ohne Abschluss)*
placement	a job, usually as a part of a course or study, which gives you experience of a particular type of work	*Praktikantenstelle*
unfair dismissal	the act of removing sb. from his job without justified reasons	*ungerechtfertigte Entlassung*
vocational training	training connected with a job	*Berufsschulausbildung*
working environment	the people and things that are around you at work	*Arbeitsumgebung*
work experience	the time that you have worked in a particular job and gained skills	*Berufserfahrung*
to work part-time	to work for part of the day or week	*halbtags/in Teilzeit arbeiten*

English word/phrase	Explanation in English	German equivalent and/or synonym(s)
Going abroad (from *Pathway, Einführungsphase*)		
to apply for a visa ['viːzə]	to make a formal request for permission to enter a foreign country	*ein Visum beantragen*

certificate of vaccination	an official document that shows a person's vaccinations/ immunization against certain diseases	*Impfpass*
cross-cultural communication	communication involving ideas from different countries/ cultures	*interkulturelle Verständigung*
cultural immersion	the state of being completely involved in a new culture	*kulturelle Verschmel-zung*
developing country/ world	a poor country/area that is trying to increase its industry and trade and improve life for its people	*Entwicklungsland*
exchange student	an arrangement in which a student attends another school or university to work or study	*Austauschschüler(in)*
first-aid courses/skills	courses that teach simple medical treatment as soon as possible to sb. that is ill or injured	*Erste-Hilfe-Kurse*
foreign currency	a different system of money to the one that is used in one's own country	*ausländische (Geld-) Währung*
to get a briefing	to be in a short meeting in which people are given instructions or information	*Instruktionen/ Anweisungen bekommen*

international driving permit	translation of one's own driving license allowing you to drive in any country for a limited period	*internationale Fahrerlaubnis/ Führerschein*
international volunteering	going abroad for volunteering	*internationaler Freiwilligendienst*
outreach programme	the activity of an organization that provides a service or advice for people in the community who would be unlikely to come to an official office	*Vor-Ort-Einsätze/ -Programme*
personal security items	items that prevent theft e. g. a money belt or a chain	*persönliche Sicherheitsvorkehrungen*
reverse culture shock	shock/difficulty that people have in adapting when they come home from a stay abroad	*Anpassungsprobleme/ Wiedereingliederungsprobleme nach einem Auslandsaufenthalt*
safety precautions	measures that sb. takes to ensure a safe environment/situation	*Sicherheitsvorkehrungen*
to settle back in	to get used to your home again	*sich wieder heimisch fühlen*
stay abroad	stay in a foreign country	*Auslandsaufenthalt*
to study abroad	to go to a school or university in a foreign country	*Auslandsstudium*
travel insurance	an insurance that helps you when you stay abroad and get ill	*Reiseversicherung*
to travel overseas	to travel to a foreign country	*eine Auslandsreise machen*

Science (Fiction) & Technology – The Modern Hydra?

English word/phrase	Explanation in English	German equivalent and/or synonym(s)
Genetic engineering		
advance	progress	*Fortschritt*
cloning	the act of producing a plant or an animal artificially from the cells of another plant or animal and thus producing sth. identical	*Klonen*
controversial	causing a lot of angry public discussion and disagreement	*kontrovers, umstritten*
to cross species	to mix two different kinds of animal breed or plant seed together	*Gattungen/Arten kreuzen*
to decode sth.	to discover the meaning of sth., esp. sth. that has been written in a code	*entschlüsseln*
to determine sth.	to discover the facts about sth.	*etwas bestimmen*
DNA	the chemical in all living things that carries genetic information	*DNA*
DNA fingerprinting	genetic fingerprinting	*genetischer Fingerabdruck*

embryonic stem cell	a basic type of cell in the body of an embryo, which can divide and develop into cells with particular functions	*Embryonenstammzellen*
a question of ethics	a question that deals with moral principles	*eine Frage der Ethik*
ethical concern	a concern that is connected with beliefs and principles about what is right and wrong	*ethische Bedenken*
gene [dʒiːn]	a unit inside a cell which controls a particular quality in a living thing	*Gen*
genetics [dʒəˈnetɪks]	the study of how the qualities of living things are passed on in their genes	*Genetik*
genetic disorder	genetic defect	*genetischer Defekt*
genetic engineering	the science of changing the information in a living being's genes	*Gentechnik*
genome	the complete set of genes in a cell or living thing	*Genom*
GM food	genetically modified food	*gentechnisch veränderte Lebensmittel*
herbicide resistant	not damaged or affected by technical substances used to kill unwanted plants	*resistent gegen Unkrautvernichtungsmittel*

to implant sth. into	to put sth. into a part of a body for medical purposes	*etw. implantieren*
to insert sth. into	to put sth. into sth. else or between two things	*etw. einfügen*
in vitro fertilization	the process by which eggs are fertilized outside of the body	*künstliche Befruchtung außerhalb des Körpers*
laboratory [lə'bɒrətri]	a room or building used for scientific research, experiments or testing	*Labor*
to manipulate [mə'nɪpjuleɪt]	to control or influence sb./sth., often in a dishonest way	*manipulieren*
to map sth.	to discover or give information about sth., esp. the way it is arranged or organized	*etw. erfassen*
to modify sth. genetically	to change the genetic code of sth.	*den genetischen Code von etw. verändern*
reproductive technology	technology connected with reproducing babies, young animals, plants	*Reproduktionstechnologie*
sample	a small amount of a substance taken from a larger amount in order to test it	*Muster, Probe*
to screen sb. for a disease	to examine sb. in order to find out if they have a particular disease	*jdn. auf eine Krankheit untersuchen*
sequence ['siːkwəns]	a set of related things which have a particular order	*Sequenz, Abfolge*

therapeutic [ˌθerəˈpjuːtɪk]	designed to help treat an illness	*therapeutisch*

English word/phrase	Explanation in English	German equivalent and/or synonym(s)
	Science & technology	
to address sth.	to deal with a certain topic	*thematisieren*
artificial intelligence	an area of study concerned with making computers copy intelligent human behaviour	*künstliche Intelligenz*
breakthrough	an important development that may lead to an agreement or achievement	*Durchbruch*
to develop sth.	to think of or produce a new product	*entwickeln; to design*
efficient	doing sth. well and thoroughly with no waste of time or money or energy	*effizient, wirksam*
exploration	an examination of sth. in order to find out about it	*Erforschung*
to explore	to examine sth. completely or carefully in order to find out more about it	*erforschen*
to generate sth.	to produce or create sth.	*erzeugen, erzielen*
to invent sth.	to make, design, or think of a new type of thing	*etwas erfinden*

invention	a useful machine, tool, instrument, etc. that has been invented	*Erfindung*
inventor	a person, who has invented sth. or whose job is to invent things	*Erfinder, Entwickler*
manufacturing	the business or industry of producing goods in factories	*Herstellung*
microelectronics [ˌmaɪkrəʊ ɪˌlekətrɒnɪks]	the design, production and use of very small electronic circuits, that are used in computers	*Mikroelektronik*
progress	the process of improving or developing, or of getting closer to finishing or achieving something	*Fortschritt*
progressive	in favour of new or modern ideas, methods, and change	*fortschrittlich*
research	the careful study of a subject	*Forschung, Recherche*
researcher	sb. who studies a subject in detail in order to discover new information	*Forscher*
robot	a machine that can perform a complicated series of tasks automatically	*Roboter*
robotics	the science of operating and designing robots	*Robotertechnik*

scientist ['saɪəntɪst]	an expert who studies or works in one or more sciences	*Wissenschaftler*
scientific (research)	involving or connected with science	*wissenschaftlich (-e Forschung)*
technological progress	a progress which is related to or involves technology	*technologischer Fortschritt*

English word/phrase	Explanation in English	German equivalent and/or synonym(s)
Utopia/dystopia		
allegory	a fictional text which has both a literal and figurative meaning	*Gleichnis, Allegorie*
allegorical	a story, painting, etc. in which the events and characters represent ideas or teach a moral lesson	*sinnbildlich*
anti-utopia	a futuristic world in which individual freedom is severely limited	*Antiutopie, Dystopie*
anti-utopian	related to an anti-utopia	*antiutopisch, dystopisch*
apocalyptic literature	literature which deals with the end of the world	*apokalyptische Literatur, Endzeit-Literatur*
authoritarian state [ɔːˌθɒrɪˈteəriən steɪt]	a state in which people are forced to obey authority and rules, even when these are wrong and unfair	*autoritärer Staat*
to be doomed	to be certain to fail or suffer	*verdammt sein*

doom	death or destruction	*Untergang, Verderben*
dystopia	a failed or fallen society	*Dystopie*
dystopian [dɪs'təʊpiən]	related to an imaginary state or place in which everything is extremely bad or unpleasant	*dystopisch*
to envision	to imagine	*sich ausmalen, sich vorstellen*
fictitious	invented by a writer	*fiktiv*
futuristic	extremely modern and unusual in appearance, as if belonging to a future time	*futuristisch*
hierarchy ['haɪərɑːki]	a system in a society or an organization, in which people are organized into different levels of importance	*Hierarchie, Rangordnung*
hierarchical	arranged in an hierarchy	*hierarchisch*
ideal society	a society without fault, a perfect society	*ideale Gesellschaft*
imaginary [ɪ'mædʒɪnəri]	existing only in your mind or imagination	*imaginär, erfunden, eingebildet*
narrative fiction	books and stories about imaginary people and events	*erzählende Literatur*
nightmare	a dream that is very frightening or unpleasant	*Albtraum*
nightmarish	frightening, horrific	*albtraumhaft, beklemmend*

oppression of people	the act of treating people unfairly or cruelly and preventing them from having opportunities and freedom	*Unterdrückung von Menschen*
science fiction	science fantasy, scientific or techno-logical speculation	*Science-Fiction*
snooper state	(*infml.*) a state that tries to find out private things about people	*Schnüffelstaat*
totalitarian state [təʊˌtæləˈteəriən steɪt]	a state in which there is only one political party that has complete power and control over the people	*totalitärer Staat*
surveillance [sɜːˈveɪləns]	the act of carefully watching a person or a place because they may be connected with crime	*Überwachung*
utopia [juːˈtəʊpiə]	an imaginary place or state in which everything is perfect	*Utopie*
utopian *(adj.)*	imaginary, almost impossible	*utopisch*
visionary [ˈvɪʒənri]	with the ability to imagine how a country, etc. will develop in the future	*visionär*

English, Englishes ... Globish – English Around the World

English word/phrase	Explanation in English	German equivalent and/or synonym(s)
	Language	
acronym	a word formed from the first letters of the words that make up the name of sth., e.g. UN (United Nations)	*Akronym, Kurzwort*
bilingual	a person with a command of two languages	*zweisprachig*
colloquial	used in conversation but not in formal speech or writing	*umgangssprachlich*
colloquialism	an expression or word used in informal conversation	*umgangssprachlicher Ausdruck*
communicative competence	a person's awareness of the rules governing the appropriate use of language in social situations	*kommunikative Fähigkeit/Kompetenz*
four-letter words	swear/curse words	*Schimpfwort, Kraftausdruck*
Globish	a simplified form of international English	*Globish*
lingua franca	a medium of communication used by people who speak different first languages	*Verkehrssprache, Lingua franca*

literary freedom	personal variation of the English language as used by writers, poets, etc.	*dichterische Freiheit*
loan/borrowing	a word from another language used in its original form	*Lehnwort*
mother tongue	the language that you first learn to speak when you are a child	*Muttersprache*
multilingual	a person with a command of several languages	*mehrsprachig*
native speaker	a speaker of a certain language as a first language	*Muttersprachler*
Netspeak	language varieties used to communicate on the Internet	*Netzjargon*
paraphrase	an alternative way of saying sth.	*Umschreibung*
phrase	a group of words that together have a particular meaning	*Wendung*
primary language	the language a person learned first, or the one he/she uses most often	*Primärsprache*
secondary language	a person's second language or one that is used less often	*Zweitsprache*
slang	informal, non-standard vocabulary	*Slang, Umgangssprache*
synonym	a word that has the same meaning as another word	*Synonym, sinnverwandtes Wort*

syntax	sentence structure	*Satzbau*
technical term	a word for a particular subject, that is difficult to understand if you do not know about that subject	*Fachbegriff*

English word/phrase	Explanation in English	German equivalent and/or synonym(s)
	English	
AE/US (abbr.)	American English	*amerikanisches Englisch*
BE (abbr.)	British English	*britisches Englisch*
bisyllabic [ˌbaɪˌsɪˈlæbɪk]	consisting of two syllables	*zweisilbig*
Black English	variety of English spoken by African-Americans	*Afroamerikanisches Englisch*
dialect [ˈdaɪəlekt]	a language variety with unique features of pronunciation, grammar and vocabulary used by with speakers with a certain regional or social background	*Dialekt, Mundart*
Englishes	international varieties of English	*Varietät einer Sprache, z. B. Dialekt, Jugendsprache, Soziolekt etc.*
EFL	English as a Foreign Language	*Englisch als Fremdsprache*
ESL	English as a Second Language	*Englisch als Zweitsprache*
monosyllabic	consisting of a single syllable	*einsilbig*

non-Standard English	informal or slang vocabulary, grammar or pronunciation	*nicht der sprachlichen Norm entsprechendes Englisch, z.B. Umgangssprache, Dialekt etc.*
official language	the language or one of the languages that is accepted by a country's government	*Amtssprache*
Pidgin (English)	a language with a reduced range of structure and vocabulary which develops among two cultures without a common language	*Pidgin-Englisch*
pronunciation	the way in which a language or a particular word or sound is pronounced	*Aussprache*
Queen's English	the 'prestige accent' known as Received Pronunciation	*englische Hochsprache*
RP	Received Pronunciation; the regionally neutral, prestige accent of British English	*britische Standardaussprache, anerkannte Aussprache*
spoken English	words and expressions mostly used in spoken English	*mündliche/gesprochene Sprache*
Standard English	a prestige variety of English, used as an institutionalized norm	*Standardenglisch*
syllable	an element of speech that acts as a unit of rhythm	*Silbe*

variety [vəˈraɪəti]	a situationally distinctive system of linguistic expression, e.g. formal, colloquial, etc.	*Abart, Spielart*
written English	words and expressions mostly used in written English	*Schriftenglisch*

English word/phrase	Explanation in English	German equivalent and/or synonym(s)
Linguistics		
capitalization	to begin a word with a capital letter	*Großschreibung*
collocation	when two or more words are often used together, e.g. fast food, a quick shower, to commit suicide, etc.	*Kollokation, gängige Wortverbindung*
consonant	a letter of the alphabet that represents a consonant sound	*Konsonant*
diphthong	a combination of two vowel sounds, e.g. the sounds [aɪ] in 'pipe'	*Doppellaut*
compound	a noun, an adjective or verb made of two or more words or joined by a hyphen, e.g. travel agent, dark-haired, etc.	*Wortverbindung*
linguistics	the science of language	*Sprachwissenschaft*
neologism [niˈɒlədʒɪzəm]	the creation of a new word	*Neologie, Neuschöpfung*

orthography	spelling	*Rechtschreibung*
phonetics	the study of how humans make, transmit and receive speech sounds	*Phonetik; Lautschrift*
phonology	the study of the sound systems of languages	*Phonologie, Lautlehre*
social variation	unique linguistic features that are related to the social background/class of speakers	*soziale Sprachvariante*
terminology	the set of technical words or expressions used in a particular subject	*Fachsprache, Terminologie*
vowel	a letter that represents a vowel sound	*Vokal*

Culture & Art – Ways of Expressing Oneself

English word/phrase	Explanation in English	German equivalent and/or synonym(s)
	Arts	
abstract painting	a painting that does not picture things or people in a realistic way	*abstraktes Gemälde*
the arts	art, music, theatre, film, literature etc. all considered together	*die Künste*
art dealer	a person that trades in art	*Kunsthändler*
artist	sb. who produces art	*Künstler*
art movements	groups of artists which have similar ideas and interests in style	*Künstlerbewegungen*
background	the things that can be seen behind the main things or people in a picture	*Hintergrund*
bright/radiant colours	intensive/glowing colours	*leuchtende Farben*
brush stroke	the way in which paint is put onto a surface with a brush	*Pinselstrich*
brush work	the way in which an artist puts paint on a picture by using a brush	*Pinselführung*
canvas	a painting done with oil paints, or the piece of cloth it is painted on	*Leinwand*

charcoal drawing	a painting drawn with a hard black substance similar to coal	*Kohlezeichnung*
colour scheme [skiːm]	a combination of colours that has been chosen for a painting	*Farbabstimmung*
to commission sth.	to order sth.	*etw. beauftragen/ anordnen;* to instruct
contemporary	existing or happening now	*zeitgenössisch*
covering application (of paint)	the act of painting e. g. a wall in a way that underlying paint or structures aren't visible anymore	*deckender Farbauftrag*
dab of colour	to put colour on something with quick light touches	*Farbtupfer*
to design sth.	to make a drawing or plan of sth. that will be made or built	*etw. gestalten*
drawing	a picture made with a pen or pencil	*Zeichnung*
etching	a picture made by printing from an etched metal plate	*Radierung*
Expressionism	art movement of the early 20th century	*Expressionismus*
expressionist	an artist who belongs to the art movement of expressionism	*Expressionist*
figurative painting	a type of art that shows objects, people, or the countryside as the really look	*darstellende Malerei*

figurative portrayal	the act of showing or describing objects or people, etc. in a picture, play book, etc.	*figürliche Darstellung*
foreground	the people, objects, etc. in a picture that seem nearest to you and form its main part	*Vordergrund*
forgery	a painting that has been copied illegally	*Fälschung;* fake
landscape	an area of countryside or land of a particular type	*Landschaft*
masterpiece	a work of art that is of very high quality	*Meisterwerk*
mixture/composition of colours	the act of mixing and using colours	*Farbmischung, Farbkomposition*
Modernism	art movement of the middle of the 20th century	*Moderne*
oil on canvas	oil painting	*Ölgemälde*
oil painting	a painting drawn with oil paints	*Ölgemälde*
painter	sb. who paints pictures	*Maler*
pastel drawing	a picture drawn with colours that are light and pale	*Pastellzeichnung*
to perform sth.	to do sth. to entertain people	*etw. vorführen/ aufführen*
performance	the act of performing a play or a piece of music, also the way sb. do performs	*Performanz, Aufführung*

performer	an artist who performs to entertain people	*Künstler/in, Darsteller/in*
performing arts	arts such as dance, music or drama	*darstellende Künste*
picture size/format	the size of a painting	*Bildformat, Bildgröße*
piece of art	sth. that has been produced by an artist	*Kunstwerk*
photographer [fə'tɒgrəfə(r)]	someone who takes photographs, esp. as a professional or as an artist	*Fotograf*
plagiarism	when someone uses another person's work and pretends that it is their own	*Plagiat, Nachahmung*
portrait	a painting, drawing, or photograph of a person	*Porträt*
print	letters, numbers, words or symbols that have been produced on paper by a machine using ink (= *Tinte)*	*Druck*
reflexion of light	the action or process of light being reflected from a surface	*Lichtreflektion*
representational painting	realistic painting	*gegenständliche Malerei (naturalistische Malerei)*
reproduction	copy of a work of art	*Reproduktion, Vervielfältigung*
sculptor	sb. who makes sculptures out of stone, wood, etc.	*Bildhauer*

shade	the dark places in a picture or painting	*Schattierung*
spatial perspective	perspective relating to the position, size, shape etc. of things	*räumliche Perspektive*
Street Art	art that is practised outside on the streets	*Straßenkunst*
to have a talent for sth.	to be good at sth.	*ein Talent für etwas haben*
three-dimensionality	an effect appearing to have three dimensions (= length, width, and height) and therefore looking real	*dreidimensionale Wirkung*
transparent/ translucent	if sth. is transparent, you can see through it very clearly	*durchscheinend*
two-dimensional (portrayal)	flat portrayal without depth, does not seem real	*flächige Darstellung*
video art	the art of filming	*Videokunst*
visual arts	art such as painting and sculpture etc. that you look at, as opposed to literature or music	*bildende Künste*
work of art	a piece of art	*Kunstwerk*
watercolour (painting)	to paint in watercolours	*Aquarell*
watercolours	a type of paint that you mix with water	*Aquarellfarbe, Wasserfarbe*

English word/phrase	Explanation in English	German equivalent and/or synonym(s)
Culture		
to award a prize to sb.	to officially give sb. sth. such as a price or money	*einen Preis verleihen*
auction [ˈɔːkʃn]	a public meeting where things are sold to the person who offers the most money for them	*Auktion, Versteigerung*
to auction sth.	to sell sth. at an auction	*etw. versteigern*
blockbuster	a book or film that is very good or successful	*Knüller, Bestseller*
box-office hit	a successful film as measured by the number of people who pay to see it	*Kassenschlager*
budget	the money that is available to a company or person	*Budget, Etat*
to cause controversy	to start a controversial discussion	*eine kontroverse Diskussion auslösen*
collection	a set of similar things that are kept or brought together because they are attractive or interesting	*Sammlung*
collector	sb. who collects things that are interesting or attractive to them	*Sammler/in*
controversial	causing disagreement or discussion	*kontrovers, umstritten*

demand for sth.	the need or desire that people have for particular goods and services	*Nachfrage nach*
failure	a lack of success in achieving or doing sth.	*Scheitern, Versagen*
flop	sth. that is not successful	*Flop, Reinfall*
funding	money that is provided by an organization for a particular purpose	*Mittel, Gelder*
to fund	to provide money for sth.	*finanzieren;* to finance
high culture	well-educated	*hohe Bildung*
mass culture	involving or intended for a very large number of people	*Massenkultur*
to nominate sb. for an award	to officially suggest sb. for an important price	*jdn. für einen Preis nominieren*
promoter	sb. who tries to encourage sth. to happen or develop	*Veranstalter/in, Förderer*
piracy ['paɪrəsi]	the crime of illegally copying sth.	*Produktpiraterie*
to promote sb./sth.	to encourage sb./sth.	*jdn./etw. fördern*
record company	a company that produces and manages the publications of singers and songwriters	*Plattenfirma*
release date	a new CD, film, video, etc. that is available to buy or see	*Erscheinungs-/ Freigabedatum*

source of revenue	source of income	*Einnahmequelle*
sponsor	supporter	*Sponsor*
state-of-the-art	using the most modern and recently developed methods, materials or knowl-edge	*auf dem neuesten Stand der Technik*
subsidy ['sʌbsədi]	money given as part of the cost of sth., to help or encourage it to happen	*Subvention*
to subsidize	to pay part of the cost of sth.	*subventionieren*

The Mass Media – Perils, Promises & Podcasts

English word/phrase	Explanation in English	German equivalent and/or synonym(s)
Media		
to be accessible	able to be reached or easily got to	*zugängig sein*
audio file	an information connected with sound stored on a computer as one unit with one name	*Audiodatei*
to bookmark a website	to record the address of a file, page on the Internet, that enables you to find it quickly	*ein Lesezeichen bei einer Internetseite setzen*
commercialization	the process of making profit from sth. and being more interested in profit than in the values/quality of sth.	*Kommerzialisierung*
compatibility	the ability of computers and programmes to be used together	*Verträglichkeit, Kompatibilität*
to cover a subject	to report on an event for TV, a newspaper, etc.	*über etw. berichten*
to design a website	to create or develop a website	*eine Internetseite erstellen*
documentary	a film giving facts about sth.	*Dokumentarfilm*
factual report	a report based on or containing facts	*Tatsachenbericht*

to have access to sth.	to have the opportunity or right to use or to see sth.	*zu etwas Zugang haben*
to infiltrate	to enter a place or organization secretly, esp. in order to get information	*unterwandern*
interactive media systems	media systems which allow information to be passed continuously and in both directions between the system/computer and the person who uses is	*interaktive Medien*
to invade sb.'s privacy	to affect sb.'s privacy in an unpleasant or annoying way	*in jds. Privatsphäre eindringen*
live coverage	a report on television or radio that is seen or heard at the same time as it is actually happening	*Direktübertragung*
to monitor sb.	to watch and check sb. over a period of time in order to see how or what they are doing	*jdn. überwachen;* to observe
on the net	on the Internet	*im Internet*
panel game	a game in which a team of people try to answer questions correctly, especially on TV or radio	*Ratespiel*
popularization	the process of making sb./sth. popular and known to a lot of people	*Popularisierung*

to post sth. online	to put sth. on a website	*im Internet veröffentlichen*
to release sth.	to publish sth.	*etw. veröffentlichen, herausgeben*
safeguard	sth. that is designed to protect sth. from harm, danger, etc.	*Schutzmaßnahme, Sicherheitsvorkehrung*
search engine	a computer program that searches the Internet for information	*Suchmaschine*
search term	a term/word, which you enter in a search engine to look after information about it on the Internet	*Suchbegriff*
self-regulation	a system that controls itself	*Selbstregulierung*
sitcom	situational comedy	*Sitcom, Fernsehkomödie*
soap (opera)	a story about the lives and problems of a group of people which is broadcast every day on television or radio	*Seifenoper*
to surf the Internet	to spend time visiting a lot of websites	*im Internet surfen*
surveillance [sɜːˈveɪləns]	the act of carefully watching a person suspected of a crime	*Überwachung*
to revolutionize sth.	to completely change the way that sth. is done	*umwälzen, revolutionieren*
source of information	the place where sb. finds information	*Informationsquelle*

virus ['vaɪrəs]	instructions that are hidden in a computer program and are designed to cause faults or destroy data	*Computervirus*

English word/phrase	Explanation in English	German equivalent and/or synonym(s)
	The press	
to appeal to sb.	to make a formal request to sb.	*jdn. ansprechen*
attention-grabbing	to attract the attention of sb. in a rather spectacular way, e. g. by very large or provocative headlines or photographs	*anreißerisch, aufsehenheischend*
balanced	keeping or showing a balance so that different things or different parts of sth. exist in equal or correct amounts	*ausgewogen, neutral*
breaking news	news that has just occurred	*Eilmeldung, Sondermeldung*
broadcasting company	a company whose business is to make and send out radio and television programmes	*Rundfunk-/Fernsehanstalt*
censorship	the act or policy of removing parts from a book, film/movie, etc. which are considered to be offensive, immoral or a political threat	*Zensur*

circulation figures	the usual number of copies of a newspaper or magazine that are regularly sold out	*Auflagenhöhe*
coverage*	the reporting of news in newspapers, radio or TV	*Berichterstattung*
to cover a subject	to report on sth.	*von etw. berichten*
classified ad	a small advertisement you put in a newspaper to buy or sell something	*Kleinanzeige*
code of ethics	a set of moral principles or rules of behaviour	*ethischer Kodex*
current affairs	events of political or social importance that are happening now	*Tagesgeschehen*
editorial	an important article in a newspaper, that expresses the editor's opinion about an item of news or an issue	*Leitartikel*
factual (information)	based on or containing facts	*Sachinformation*
freedom of the press	the legal right to write or say what you want	*Pressefreiheit*
gossip	informal talk or stories about other people's private lives, often including unkind or untrue remarks	*Klatsch(presse)*
hard news	facts, factual information	*Fakten*

letter to the editor*	a letter sent to a publication, e.g. a magazine or (online) newspaper, about issues of concern from its readers	*Leserbrief an den Herausgeber*
objective	not influenced by personal feelings or opinions	*objektiv, sachlich*
private sector broadcaster	private broadcasting companies	*private Fernsehanstalt*
public sector broadcaster	public broadcasting companies	*öffentlich-rechtliche Fernsehanstalt*
to publish	to produce a book, magazine, CD-ROM, etc. and sell it to the public; to print a letter, an article, etc. in a newspaper or a magazine	*veröffentlichen*
popular newspaper/ tabloid*	a newspaper with small pages, short simple reports and a lot of pictures and stories about famous people, often thought as less serious than other newspapers	*Boulevardzeitung*
quality newspaper/ broadsheet*	a newspaper printed on a larger size, generally considered more serious than smaller newspapers	*seriöse Zeitung*
sensationalist [sen'seɪʃənəlɪst]	seeking to attract people's emotions	*sensationslüstern, effekthascherisch*
subjective	based on your own ideas and opinions rather than facts	*subjektiv*

English word/phrase	Explanation in English	German equivalent and/or synonym(s)
Communication		
addressee [ˌædre'siː]	a person that sth. is addressed to	*Adressat*
to address sth.	to directly say or write sth. to sb.	*etw. ansprechen*
to communicate with sb.	to exchange information, news, ideas, etc. with sb.	*kommunizieren*
communications systems	systems, that are used to send information, especially telephones, radio, computers, etc.	*Kommunikationsmittel*
data ['deɪtə, 'dɑːtə]	facts or information, especially when examined and used to find out things or to make decisions	*Daten*
data theft	the act of stealing data	*Datendiebstahl*
to distribute sth. via (the Internet)	to send information using a particular way/method	*etw. (über das Internet) verbreiten*
means of communication	a method or way of communicating	*Kommunikationsweise*
means of persuasion	a method or way of making sb. do or believe sth.	*Überzeugungsmethode*
to process sth.	to deal officially with a document, request, etc. in the usual way; to deal with information using a computer	*etw. verarbeiten*
to respond to sth.	to react to sth. or to answer to sth.	*antworten, reagieren*

to transfer data	to move information from one place to another	*Daten übertragen*
wireless communication	a system of sending and receiving signals that does not use wires	*drahtlose Kommunikation*
word processing	the use of a computer to create, store and print a piece of text	*Textverarbeitung*

Shakespeare – Cult and Culture?!

English word/phrase	Explanation in English	German equivalent and/or synonym(s)
Shakespeare's theatre		
bawdiness [ˈbɔːdines]	the act of making humorous remarks about sex that are funny and often noisy	*Derbheit*
censorship	the practise or system of censoring and controlling sth.	*Zensur*
to deal with a theme	to be about a theme	*ein Thema behandeln, von einem Thema handeln*
dramatist	someone who writes plays, esp. serious ones	*Dramatiker*
first edition	first printed version of a play	*Erstausgabe*
gallery	upstairs areas in the theatre	*Balkon, Empore*
groundlings	poorest theatre-goers who had to stand in the open yard in front of the stage	*unter freiem Himmel stehende Zuschauer, Stehplätze*
history play	historical drama	*historisches Schauspiel*
playwright	writer of plays	*Dramatiker*
to produce a play	to make a play	*ein Schauspiel produzieren*
repertory	collection of plays, pieces of music, etc. that a performer or theatre company has learnt and can perform	*Repertoire, Repertoire-theater*

theatre company	group of people (actors, playwright, etc.) that work together at a theatre	*Theaterensemble, Schauspieltruppe*
the wooden O	nickname given to the Globe Theatre because of its circular shape	*„Das hölzerne O" (Spitzname des Globe Theaters aufgrund seiner runden Form)*

English word/phrase	Explanation in English	German equivalent and/or synonym(s)
Shakespeare's language		
anon	soon	*bald*
bard	a person who writes poems	*Dichter, Barde*
belied	told lies about	*täuschen, lügen*
belike	probably	*vielleicht*
betimes	in time	*beizeiten*
blank verse	poetry that has a regular rhythm, usually ten syllables and five stresses, but which does not rhyme	*Blankvers (reimloser, fünfhebiger, jambischer Vers)*
bondman	slave	*Sklave, Leibeigene/r*
buss	kiss	*Kuss*
cozenage	cheating	*betrügen, Betrug*
crowns/crownets	kings/princes	*Könige/Prinzen*
doomsday	day of death	*Todestag*
dost	does	*machen, tun*
doublet	Elizabethan jacket	*kurze, enge Jacke, die europäische Männer vom 15. bis ins 17. Jh. trugen*
fancy	love	*Liebe, Vorliebe*

fell	cruel, brutal, savage	*grausam, brutal*
figurative	symbolic	*symbolisch, bildhaft*
giving him the lie	tricking him	*jdn. täuschen/reinlegen*
hath	has	*haben*
luxurious	lustful	*lüstern*
methinks	I believe, I think	*ich glaube, ich denke*
metaphorical	connected with or containing metaphors	*methaphorisch*
mistress	the female head of the house: a woman who is in a position of authority or control	*Herrin, die Frau des Hauses*
paragon	ideal of excellence	*Vorbild, Muster*
play on words	an amusing use of a word or phrase that has two meanings	*Wortspiel*
pun	play on words	*Wortspiel*
prose	writing that is not poetry	*Prosa (ungebundene Rede)*
redress	justice	*Gerechtigkeit*
strumpeted	made a prostitute	*sich oder jdn. prostituieren*
sudden	violent	*gewalttätig*
tall	brave	*mutig, tapfer*
thee	you	*du/Sie/Ihr*
thine	yours	*deine(r, s), Eure(r, s), Ihre(r, s)*
thou [ðaʊ]	you – used a) by lower classes talking to each other, b) by superiors talking to inferiors, c) for special intimacy, d) by a character is talking to sb. absent	*du*

thy	your	*dein(e), euer/eure, ihr(e)*
thyself	yourself	*dich*
undone	ruined	*zerstört, ruiniert*
wast	was	*war*
will	wish, sexual desire	*Wille, sexuelles Verlangen*
withal *(arch.)*	therewith	*damit*
wont	accustomed	*gewohnt, üblich*
woo't	would you	*würdest du, würden Sie, würdet Ihr*

English word/phrase	Explanation in English	German equivalent and/or synonym(s)
Elizabethan England		
age of (scientific) invention	a particular period in history (16th/17th century)	*neues (wissenschaftliches) Zeitalter, Zeitalter der Erfindungen*
alchemy	a half-science trying to find a way to turn base metals into gold	*Zauberei, Magie*
astrology	a half-science that believed that the constellations of the sun, moon and stars influenced man's character and fate	*Astrologie*
bad witches	women who intended to harm people in the name of Satan and with the assistance of servant demons	*böse Hexen*
geo-centric universe	the belief that the earth was at the centre of the universe	*geozentrisches Universum (Erde als Mittelpunkt)*

good witches	wise old women who helped their neighbours, gave them advice or told them their fortunes	*gute Hexen, weise alte Frauen*
Reformation	new ideas in religion in 16th-century Europe that led to attempts to reform the Roman Catholic Church and to the formation of the Protestant Churches	*Reformation (wörtl. Erneuerung)*
Renaissance [rɪˈneɪsns]	the period in Europe during the 14th, 15th and 16th centuries when people became interested in the ancient cultures of Greece and Rome	*Renaissance (Neuzeit)*
the Spanish Armada	a fleet of Spanish ships that tried to conquer England in 1588 and was defeated by Elizabeth's I navy	*die spanische Armada (Kriegsflotte)*
superstition	belief in supernatural forces	*Aberglaube*
Tudor	connected with the time when the kings and queens of the Tudor family ruled England (1485–1603)	*Tudor (royaler Familienname)*
voyages of discovery	e.g. Columbus, Magellan, etc. who sailed across the oceans to discover new countries and continents	*Entdeckungsreise(n)*

The European Union

The European Union (EU) is an **economic and political union** of 27 member states (ca. 500 million citizens) that has developed a single market **ensuring free movement of people, goods, services and capital**. The EU operates through supranational and intergovernmental negotiations and treaties between the member states. Economically the EU generates ca. 20 % of the gross world product.

History

1957	**Rome Treaty** creates the European Economic Community (EEC) as a customs union members: Belgium, France, Italy, Luxembourg, the Netherlands, West Germany
1979	first direct democratic elections to the **European Parliament**
1985	**Schengen Agreement** creates open borders without passport control between most member states
1986	the European flag is first used
1990	after German reunification, (former) East Germany joins the community
1993	in the **Maastricht Treaty**, the European Union is formally established
2002	the **Euro** is introduced as European currency and replaces national currencies in twelve of the member states

Fundamental rights

- In 2009, the **Lisbon Treaty** gave legal effect to the **Charter of Fundamental Rights of the European Union** which is a catalogue of fundamental (human) rights which were derived from the constitutional traditions of the member states (e.g. **Article 1:** Human dignity is inviolable. It must be respected and protected; **Article 2:** Everyone has the right to life. No one shall be condemned to the death penalty, or executed.).

Important EU institutions

- the **European Council** is the EU's supreme political authority; it defines the EU's political agenda and strategies
- the **European Commission** is the EU's executive branch and responsible for its legislation
- the **European Parliament** (in Strasbourg) forms half of the EU's legislature; the members of the European Parliament are directly elected by the EU citizens every five years
- the **Council of the European Union** is the other half of the EU's legislature; in addition to legislative functions it also has executive functions, e. g. the Common Foreign and Security Policy
- the **Court of Justice of the European Union** interprets and applies the treaties and the law of the EU
- the **European Central Bank** administers the monetary policy of the 16 member states taking part in the **Eurozone**; it is one of the world's most important central banks

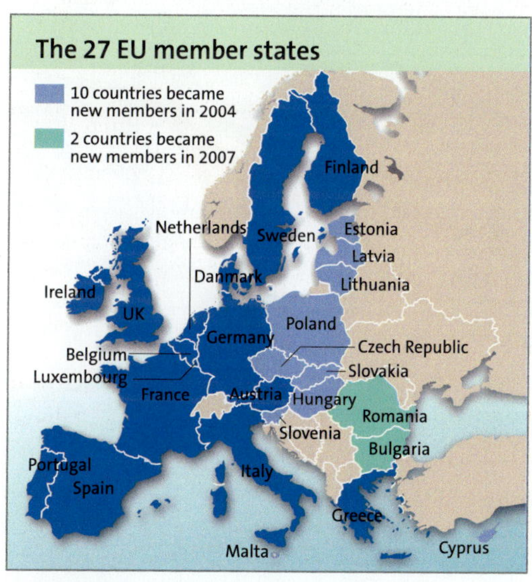

➔ Focus on Vocab, pp. 5 ff.

The British Empire

The system of triangle trading

British involvement with the **triangular trade began with the colonization of America in 1607 and the West Indies in 1623**. The chief British ports were London, Liverpool, Bristol and Glasgow.

Triangular trade is a historical term that refers to trade among three ports or regions and countries. The best-known triangular trading system is the **transatlantic trade** that operated from the seventeenth until the early nineteenth century, carrying manufactured goods, raw materials, cash crops – and slaves – between West Africa, the Caribbean and American colonies and the European colonial powers.

The **use of African slaves was fundamental** to growing crops such as cotton and tobacco, which were then exported to Europe. In

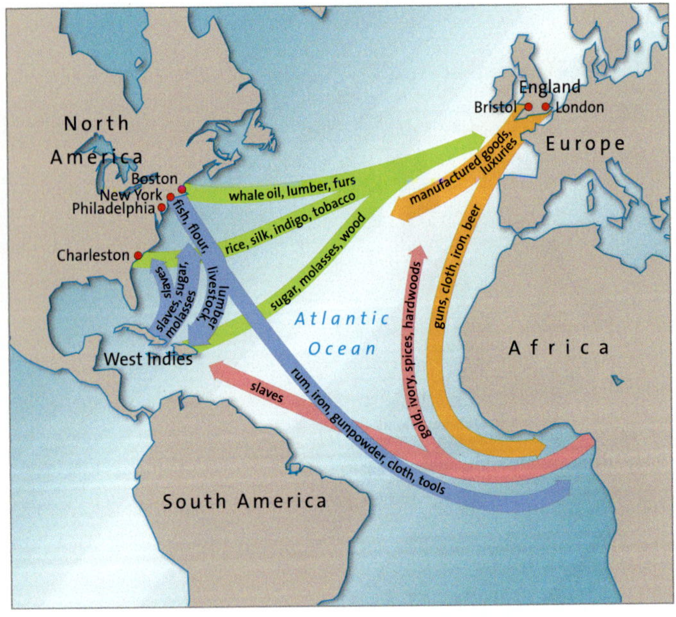

turn, European goods were used to buy slaves from traders in Africa or the Caribbean. The slaves were transported to the Americas on the sea lane, the so-called middle passage, which was a horrible journey during which many slaves died of diseases and maltreatment. **Slave trade was started in 1501** by Portuguese and Spanish traders; in 1807, the UK Parliament passed a bill that officially abolished the trading of slaves, but there was still illegal slave trade across the Atlantic Ocean that was practiced until the second half of the nineteenth century. There are an estimated 27 million victims of slavery worldwide today.

The British Empire in 1750

The British Empire in the 1750s (the blue shaded areas) traded goods worth £17 million, £8.7 million in exports and £8.3 million in imports. Britain's trade grew enormously because Britain gained control over many different parts of the world. The wish for expansion and the need for raw materials during the **Industrial Revolution** caused a series of overseas wars among several European countries such as France, Spain and Holland. However, one of the first British trading companies, the **East India Company**, founded in 1600 during the reign of Elizabeth I, and the **Virginia Company**, founded by her successor James I, which was the basis for the first North American colony, the **Jamestown Colony in 1607**, formed the foundations of the growth and rise of the British Empire. Many colonies began as trading centres or were founded to protect a trade route, and were run for the profit of the mother country. The wealthiest area in the early days of the Empire was the **West Indies** due to large profits from sugar cane and tobacco. Slaves were brought to the West Indies to work on the plantations.
The map shows the variety of goods that Britain imported from all over the world that greatly influenced the British economy and people's lives in the **mother country**.

→ Focus on Vocab, pp. 5 ff.

The British Empire in 1900

Starting in 1801 the expanding empire was managed from London by the **Colonial Office**. District officers and civil servants were sent out to administer the colonies on behalf of Britain. Regular **imperial conferences** were held in Britain to discuss matters of general concern, such as trade, defence and foreign policy.

India was controlled for many years by the wealthy **East India Company**, roads and railroads were built to make trade easier, a **Governor-General** was put in charge, and British troops and civil servants were sent to the region. In 1858, following the Indian Mutiny, India was placed under the direct control of the British government and a **viceroy** replaced the Governor-General. British influence in India had expanded from a few trading stations into the **Raj** (= British rule). In 1876, **Queen Victoria** was proclaimed **Empress of India**. India brought Britain great wealth and strategic advantage, and was called the 'jewel in the crown of the Empire'. Local Indian rulers were allowed to remain in power provided they were loyal to the viceroy. Many British people spent years working in India as civil servants, engineers, police officers, etc. and took their families with them. The second period of empire-building took place in the late nineteenth century. The British Empire was at its largest and most powerful around 1920, when about 25 % of the world's population lived under British rule and over a quarter of the land in the world belonged to Britain. It was said that it was an empire **'on which the sun never sets'**, and the value of exports and imports was £970 million. At that time Britain was one of the

The Brighton Pavillion was built in 'Hindoo' style in the early nineteenth century.

greatest economic and political powers in the world. It was also thought by some people to be a moral obligation and destiny to govern poorer, less advanced countries and to pass on European culture to the native inhabitants. This was what Rudyard Kipling called the 'white man's burden'.

Britain did not only import foreign goods; there was also a great influence of foreign ideas, especially from India.

In the eighteenth century curry recipes and the famous 'mulligatawny soup' (the Tamil word for 'pepper-water') appeared in England. Indian designs influenced art and architecture, and polo, snooker and billiards, games which were played by British soldiers in India, were 'exported' to Britain.

→ Focus on Vocab, pp. 5 ff.

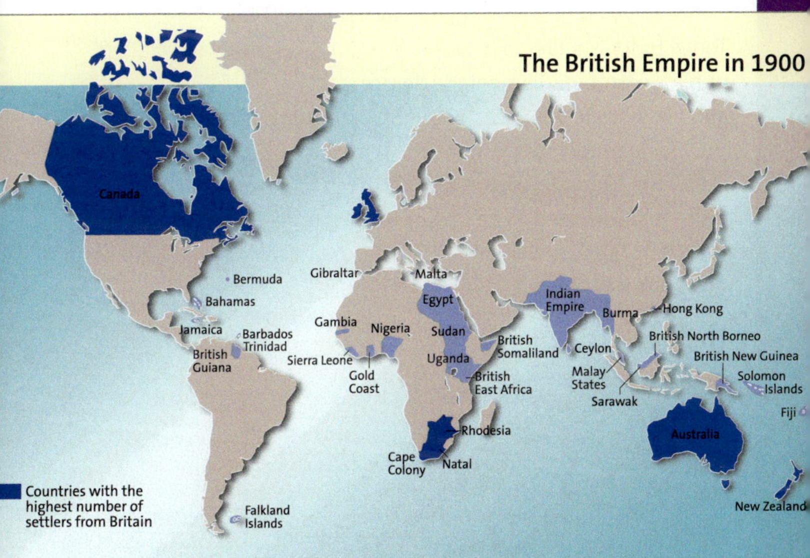

India: From "Crown Jewel of the Empire" to "the World's Largest Democracy"

With its 1.18 billion people, India, officially **the Republic of India**, is the second-most populous country in the world and the world's largest democracy. In its long history, India has always been known for its commercial and cultural wealth and diversity. Today India is a federal constitutional republic with a parliamentary democracy and consists of 28 states and 7 union territories. Head of State is the President of India, but the most executive power is exercised by the Prime Minister, who is also the head of government.

India's national emblem, the Lion of Sarnath, third century B. C.

India's flag, the Tricolour, with the navy blue wheel with 24 spokes (= Ashoka's Dharma Chakra). Each spoke depicts one hour of the day and portrays the prevalence of righteousness all 24 hours.

India is considered to be one of the fastest-growing economies in the world and is well known for its pluralistic, multilingual and multi-ethnic society.

History

Third cent. B. C.	**Ashoka the Great** unites most of South Asia
320–550 A. D.	A. D. the **Gupta dynasty** is considered to be the **Golden Age of India**; extensive inventions and discoveries in science, technology, art, literature, religion and philosophy were the foundation of the **Hindu culture**
1526–1857	age of the **Mughal Empire**; Mughal Emperors control most of the Indian subcontinent by means of a highly centralized administration

16th cent.	European powers establish trading posts
1616	the **British East India Company** is founded
1856	the British East India Company controls most of India
1857	**Indian Mutiny:** native soldiers employed by the British Army rebel against racial injustice and inequities; as a consequence civilian rebellions follow ➔ the East India Company is dissolved and India is directly governed by the Crown ➔ **British Rule/Raj**
1885	the **Indian National Congress** is founded and developed into one of the largest democratic political parties in the world; it is a major force in the struggle against British rule in India
1920s	the Indian National Congress adopts **Gandhi's ideas of non-violent civil disobedience and resistance**, which later leads to the **Quit India Movement** which is also led by Gandhi
1947	the **Indian Independence Act** leads to the dissolution of the British Indian Empire
15 Aug. 1947	India gains independence; **Partition of India** into two independent states: the **Dominion of Pakistan** (later Islamic Republic of Pakistan and People's Republic of Bangladesh) and the **Union of India** (later Republic of India)
1948	**Mahatma Gandhi is assassinated** by a Hindu fanatic
1948/1965/ 1971/1999	**Indo-Pakistan wars** over disputed territory in Kashmir and Jammu
1974	first **nuclear test explosion** under the codename "Smiling Buddha" (five further tests in 1998)
1991	economic liberalization and major reforms initiated by Prime Minister Rajiv Gandhi
2005	the **Right to Information Act** ensures the right to information for citizens
2009	the **Right to Education Bill** provides free and compulsory education for children between 6 and 14; it requires all private schools to reserve 25 % of seats for children from poor families

Great Britain – A Multicultural Society

Immigration and minorities in Great Britain

People have been coming to Britain for centuries, but immigration only became an issue in the 1960s.

After World War II, Britain needed more workers and admitted citizens of Commonwealth countries without restriction. Many came from the Caribbean and from India, Pakistan and Bangladesh. They found work in hospitals, in the textile industry and in the public transport system, though most jobs were poorly paid. **Nearly 500,000 Commonwealth citizens came to Britain before 1962**, many of whom were later joined by their families. When there were no longer enough jobs, **the Commonwealth Immigrants Act (1962)** was passed to restrict the number of immigrants entering Britain. In the following years, several more acts were passed, further restricting the right of foreigners to live in Britain. **Immigration is now strictly controlled**. Normally, only people from the European Union and certain Commonwealth citizens can get permission to live in Britain. Britain now accepts about 50,000 immigrants every year.

After periods of racism and violent demonstrations in the 1960s and 1970s, Britain has been making great efforts to integrate people from ethnic minorities into local communities and to develop a multicultural society based on equality and acceptance.

→ Focus on Vocab, pp. 5 ff.

Statistical data about minorities and population trends in Britain

The country of origin of people living in Great Britain, 2001 (%)

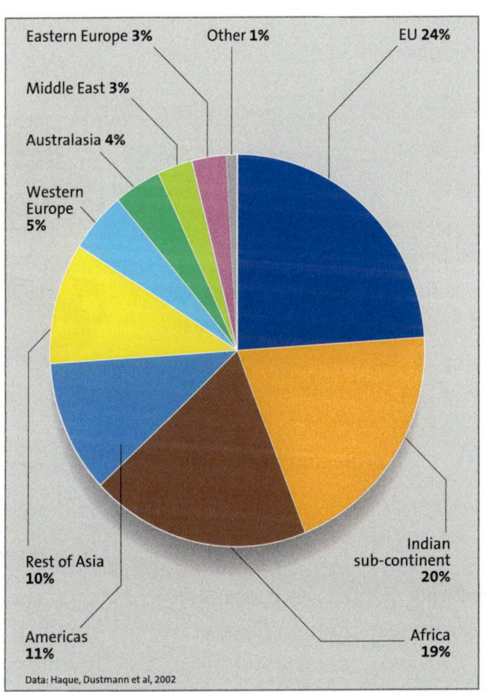

The non-white population of Great Britain, 1951 – 2001

Year	Non-white population
1951	30,000 (est.)
1961	400,000 (est.)
1971	1.4 million
1981	2.1 million
1991	3.0 million
2001	4.6 million

Data: for 1951 and 1961, Spencer (1997); for 1971, Lornas (1973); for 1981, Amin & Richardson (1992); for 1991 and 2001, Office for National Statistics and General Register Office for Scotland

American Beliefs and Values

Although there have been significant shifts in societal concepts and traditions, the following ideals, beliefs and values continue to be some of the most important in American culture.

Fundamental, inalienable and God-given rights

- **Liberty:** personal and religious freedom
- **Pursuit of happiness:**
  - individuality/individual ways of pursuing one's dreams and realizing one's goals
  - (personal and material) success and wealth
  - optimism and belief in "anticipated success"
- **Equality:** equal rights for men and women/equal rights for people from different ethnicities and social backgrounds
- **Life:** leading a secure life protected by the law, government and military

Patriotism

- importance of **national symbols** (e.g. the Statue of Liberty, the Declaration of Independence, the Constitution, the U.S. flag, the National Anthem, etc.)
- strong identification with one's nationality and **pride in being American**

Puritanism/Protestant work ethic

- the **Puritan belief that hard work, thrift, discipline, self-improvement and responsibility** lead to worldly success and prosperity and that this is a sign of God's benevolence and grace
- continuous and active participation in society and entrepreneurial endeavors
- believing that one is exceptional, **a member of "God's chosen people"**, following a divine providence (→ **Manifest Destiny**)

- belief in authority as a means of protecting the personal rights of the people

The American Dream

- the phrase "American Dream" was first expressed by the American historian and writer **James Truslow Adams in 1931**, describing a set of complex beliefs, promises of religious and personal freedom and opportunities for prosperity and success, as well as political and social expectations
- its basic underlying concept has roots in the **Declaration of Independence of 1776** which refers to basic human rights such as **"Life, Liberty and the Pursuit of Happiness"** which are **"inalienable"** and God-given and based on the assumption that "all [people] are created equal"

An open and dynamic society

- being generally open to new ideas and inventions (➔ progress)
- being generally open to immigrants of any nationality, provided they contribute positively to the country
- different concepts of how to integrate immigrants:
  a) the **melting pot** image: people are "melted together", i. e. they are expected to give up their original culture and identity and are "transformed" into a homogeneous "American culture"
  b) the **salad bowl** image: national, ethnic and cultural patterns/habits are kept distinct by the immigrants while they are rather loosely integrated into the "American culture"

➔ Focus on Vocab, pp. 24 f.

An Uncle Sam wind wheel toy for children

Minorities in the USA

Immigration into the United States of America and minorities living in the USA

The English went to North America from the late sixteenth century; Spain sent people to the southern part of the region and many Dutch and Germans also went over. When the U. S. became independent, it was written into the **Constitution** that there could be no limits on immigration until 1808. **The main period of immigration was between 1800 and 1917.** Early in this period, many more immigrants arrived from Britain and Germany, and many Chinese went to California. Later, the main groups were Italians, Irish, Eastern Europeans and Scandinavians. Many Jews came from Germany and Eastern Europe. Just before World War I, there were nearly a million new immigrants per year. Most Americans have a clear idea of what life was like for the immigrants: They left home because they were poor and thought they would have better opportunities in the U. S. Many immigrants came to New York and Boston, and **Ellis Island**, near New York, became famous as a receiving station.

The **Immigration Act of 1917**, and other laws that followed it, limited the number of immigrants who could settle in the U. S. and established quotas based on their country of origin. Since then, immigration has been limited to a few people who are selected for an **immigrant visa**, commonly called a green card. Hispanics and Asians now make up the largest groups of immigrants. **The Immigration and Naturalization Service** (INS) is responsible for issuing visas. It also tries to prevent people from crossing the borders and entering the U. S. illegally.

→ Focus on Vocab, pp. 24 f.

Ethnic minorities in the USA (US census of 2000)

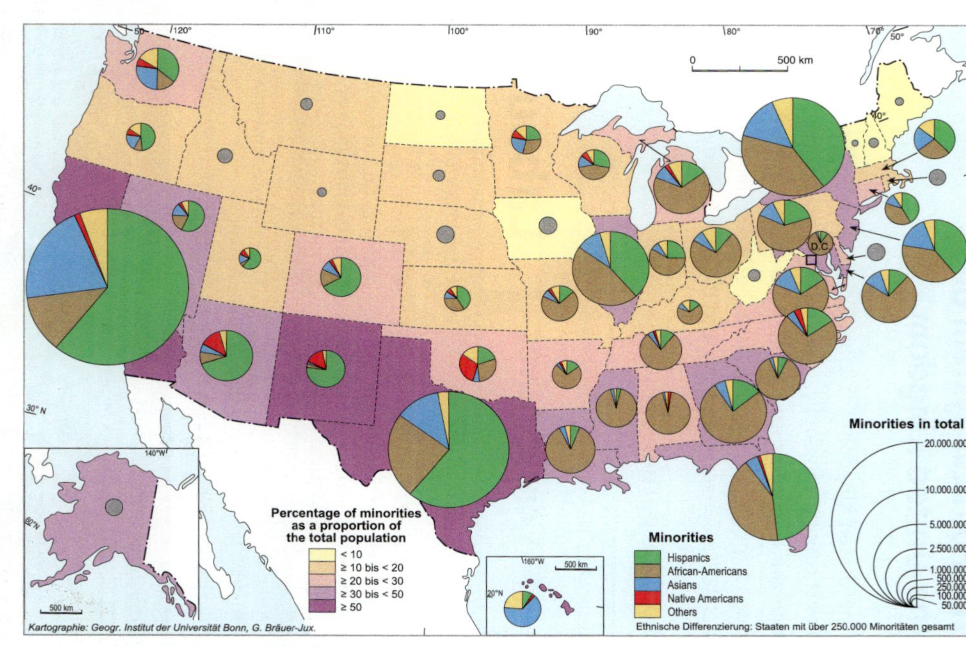

The Political System of the United Kingdom

The **United Kingdom** (of Great Britain and Northern Ireland) is **a constitutional monarchy**, in which the **monarch is the head of state and the Prime Minister is the head of government**. The UK has been a multi-party system since the 1920s, the two largest parties being the Conservative Party and the Labour Party.

Political parties

The Conservative Party	Labour Party

• centre-right • conservatism • British Unionism (against Scottish and Welsh independence) • opposition to the Euro, strong defense of Pound Sterling • Eurosceptic position • free-market policy • criticism of Labour's state multiculturalism	• left to centre-left • democratic socialist party • supports government intervention in the economy • for redistribution of wealth • advocates increased rights for workers • favours an extended welfare state • support of multiculturalism

The debating chamber of the British House of Commons in the Palace of Westminster, London

The U.K. system of government (separation of powers)

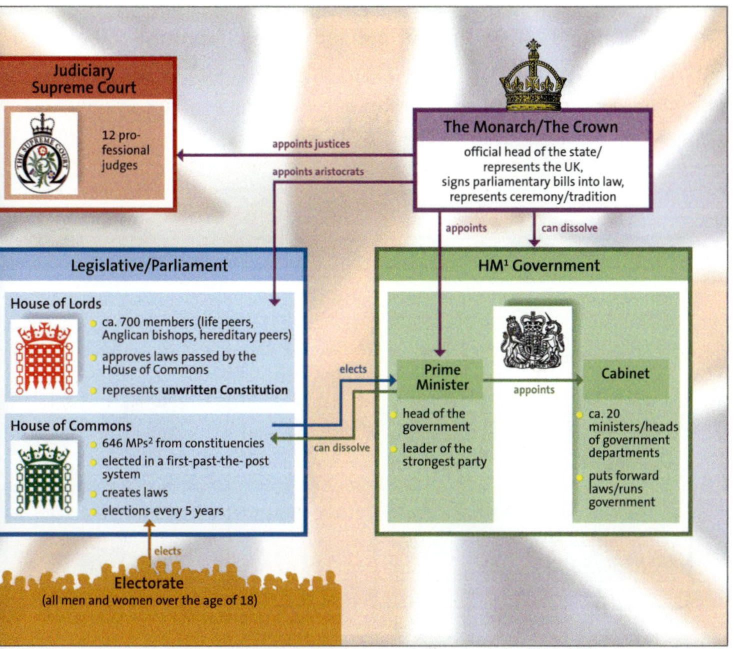

→ Focus on Vocab, pp. 46 ff.

[1] **HM** *(abbr.)* Her/His Majesty's – [2] **MP** *(abbr.)* Member of Parliament

The Political System of the United States

The U.S. system of government (checks and balances)

The United States Constitution demands a **separation of power**. Each branch of government exercises power over each of the other branches. This prevents any one branch from becoming too powerful.

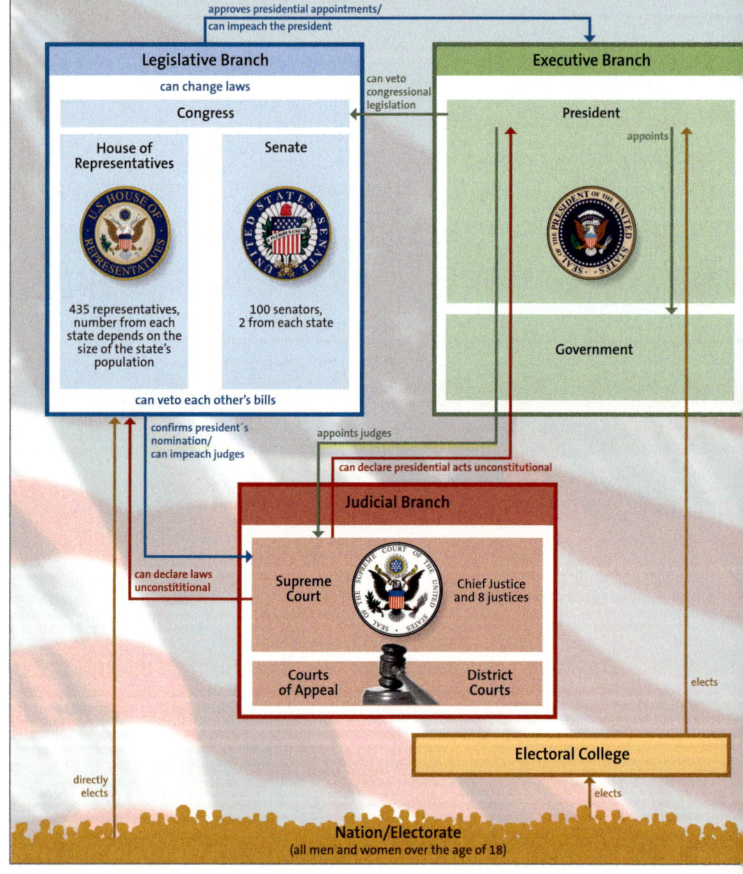

The United States has a **first-past-the-post voting system** in which the highest polling candidate is given all the votes and elected. Most states require citizens who wish to vote to be **officially registered**. Every **legal citizen over the age of 18**, regardless of ethnicity or gender, **has the right to vote**. Voting is carried out by **free and secret ballot**, in which the voters cast a **ballot (paper)** in a **ballot box** or via (electronic) **voting machines** in **polling places**, or via mail ballots.

→ Focus on Vocab, pp. 46 ff.

United States Capitol, the meating place of the US Congress

Political parties

In 1787, America's founders expected constitutional provisions such as the separation of power, checks and balances, federalism and indirect election of the president by an electoral college would deter the formation of parties. However, **in 1800 the US became the first nation to develop organized political parties** which had executive power. Since the 1860s, the Republican and Democratic parties have dominated American politics. In a 2006 Gallup Poll, ca. 59 percent of Americans identified themselves as either Republicans or Democrats.

Those people claiming to be independent normally have partisan leanings.

Democratic Party	Republican Party
• evolved from the party of Thomas Jefferson, formed before 1800 • is considered to be more liberal • believes that government has an obligation to provide social and economic programs • favours a higher taxation of the rich • has a stronger obligation to environmental engagement	• was established in the 1850s by Abraham Lincoln and others who opposed slavery • is considered to be more conservative • tends to believe that social and economic programs are too costly to taxpayers • encourages private enterprise • believes that a strong private sector makes citizens less dependent on government

The election process

- the US Constitution stipulates that **a presidential election is to be held once every four years**
- in February of the election year, the parties nominate candidates in so-called state primaries and caucuses (*US, Gremium, Ausschuss*)

- at national party conventions, usually held in the summer, **state delegates vote for the party's presidential candidate**
- on election day (usually the first Tuesday following the first Monday in November) every citizen has an opportunity to vote in **a process of indirect popular election known as the electoral college**, in which the number of electors is based on the population of the state
- these electors assemble following election day, cast their ballots and officially select the next president
- the Constitution mandates that **Senators be elected directly by the voters of their state** once every six years
- the **members of the House of Representatives are also elected directly by the voters** of their state every two years

The inauguration of the president

- the president-elect and the vice president-elect **take the oath of office** and are inaugurated on 20 January
- over the years, the inauguration has been expanded to a daylong event, including the oathtaking ceremony, parades, speeches and balls
- traditionally, the sworn-in president delivers a speech, the so-called **inaugural address**, in which he inspires hope for the future and outlines fundamental plans and objectives

"I … do solemnly swear that I will faithfully execute the office of President of the United States, and will to the best of my ability, preserve, protect, and defend the Constitution of the United States."

→ Focus on Vocab, p. 46 ff.

The United Nations

The **United Nations Organization** (UNO, UN) was **founded in 1945 to replace the League of Nations** in order **to stop wars** between countries and as **a platform for international dialogue**. It contains multiple subsidiary organizations with diverse functions to carry out the UN's missions. Today, about 192 nations belong to the UN. When nations become a member of the UN, they agree to accept the obligations of **the UN Charter**, which states the **four basic purposes of the UN**:

- to maintain **international peace and security**
- to develop **friendly relations among nations**
- to be a centre for **harmonizing the actions of nations**
- to cooperate in **solving international problems** and promoting **respect for human rights**

The organization of the United Nations

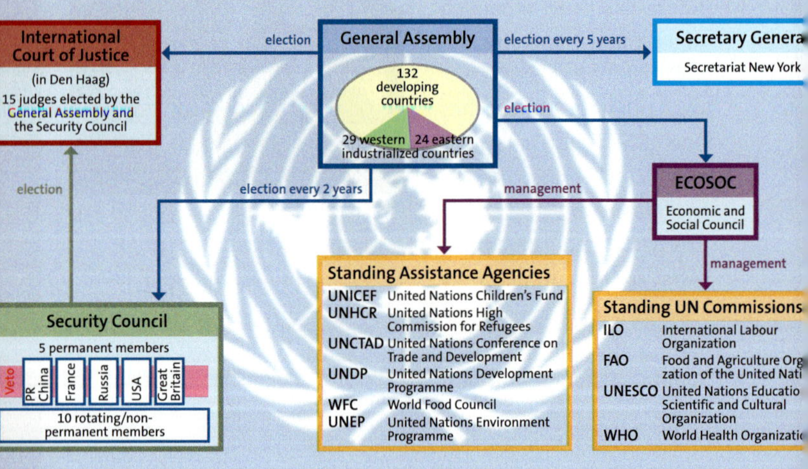

Global issues on the UN Agenda

- Africa
- Ageing
- Agriculture
- AIDS
- Atomic Energy
- Children
- Climate Change
- Culture
- Decolonization
- Demining
- Development Corporation
- Persons with Disabilities
- Disarmament
- Drugs and Crime
- Education
- Elections
- Energy
- Environment
- Family
- Food
- Governance
- Health
- Human Rights
- Human Settle-ments
- Humanitarian and Disaster Relief Assistance
- Indigenous People
- Information Communications Technology
- Intellectual Property
- International Finance
- Iraq
- Labour
- International Law
- Oceans and the Law of the Sea
- Least Developed Countries
- The Millenium UN General Assembly – The Goals
- Questions of Palestine
- Peace and Security
- Population
- Refugees
- Science and Technology
- Social Development
- Outer Space
- Statistics
- Sustainable Development
- Terrorism
- Trade and Development
- Volunteerism
- Water
- Women
- Youth

www.un.org/issues

→ Focus on Vocab, pp. 46 ff.

Sculpture in front of the UN headquarters in New York

(Global) Economy

Historical roots

- **early "world economies"** like **Phoenicia** (1200–800 B.C.), the **Roman Empire** (510 B.C.–500 A.D.), the **Silk Road** (1st century) and the **British East India Company** (founded in 1608) establish an international network of trading routes and found commercial outposts
- **inventions and discoveries** of the late **Middle Ages** and **Renaissance** enable people **in Europe** to sail and **travel longer distances** and become less dependable on weather conditions (e.g. 13th cent.: magnetic compass, mechanical clock, spectacles/lenses, scales for weighing; 16th/17th cent.: pocket watch, thermometer, telescope) ➔ international trading and exchange of goods is fostered
- **the discovery of new continents** and their subsequent conquest in the 16th and 17th centuries gives European countries access to natural resources and labour
- the **Industrial Revolution**, starting with the invention of James Watt's steam engine, enables the industrialized mass production of goods which is based on the constant input of resources, e.g. from overseas colonies
- in the **19th century colonialism and imperialism** is at its peak, leading to the growth of Western economic power and dominance, but also dramatic and long-lasting social and economic problems in the colonised countries which linger to this day

Global players – and the consequences

- **multinational companies** (or mega corporations) play an important role in the international economy: they often have powerful influence on local economies, international relations and even politics (➔ lobbying)
- **many multinational companies are criticized** due to lax environmental standards, bad labour standards (e.g. sweatshops in

developing countries, control of tariffs → unfair wages), marginalization of local businesses/markets

- many multinationals hold **patents** (e. g. Siemens, Adidas) in order to prevent the rise of competitors
- examples of **influential multinational corporations** are: Exxon-Mobil, Wal-Mart, McDonald's, General Electric, Boeing, Microsoft and British Petrol
- the United Nations declare **2005 the International Year of Microcredit**; microloans are designed to spur entrepreneurship in developing countries and gain acceptance in the mainstream finance industry as a source of future growth

Energy – reserves and consumption

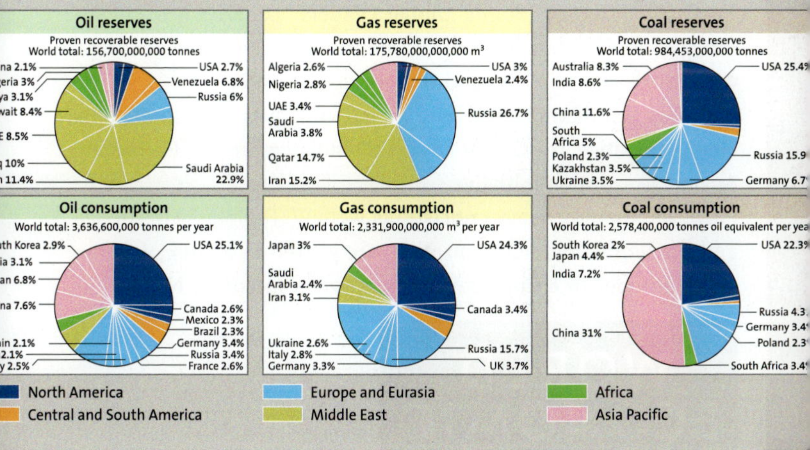

World Trade

World Economic Forum

The **World Economic Forum** (WEF), founded in 1971, is a Swiss nonprofit foundation that meets annually in Davos, and **brings together international business and political leaders, intellectuals and journalists to discuss pressing global issues**.

Besides its economic focus, the annual meeting has become a neutral platform for political leaders to resolve political differences. In 2008, Microsoft founder Bill Gates gave a keynote speech on "creative capitalism", which combines generating profits and solving the world's inequities by using market forces to address the needs of the poor worldwide. The participants are considered a global elite – a think tank of internationally-oriented experts, including a group of "Young Global Leaders" consisting of under-forty-year-old leaders from all around the world and representing a wide range of disciplines and sectors.

WEF has also **launched several global initiatives**, e.g. the **Global Health Initiative**, the **Global Education Initiative** and the **Partnering Against Corruption Initiative**.

However, there is heavy criticism as well: WEF, along with the G8 and the World Trade Organisation, are viewed as a "mix of pomp and platitude" by anti-globalisation activists and many NGOs.

Further economic forums

- **The Group of Eight (G8):** France, Germany, Italy, Japan, the United Kingdom, the United States, Canada and Russia

This group has occasionally been expanded, e.g.:

- **Outreach Five (O5):** plus Brazil, China, India, Mexico and South Africa
- **Group of Twenty (G20):** the 20 major economies of Africa, North America, South America, East Asia, South Asia, Southeast Asia, Western Asia, Eurasia, Europe and Oceania; the group meets semi-annually, and the last meeting took place in Seoul in November 2010.

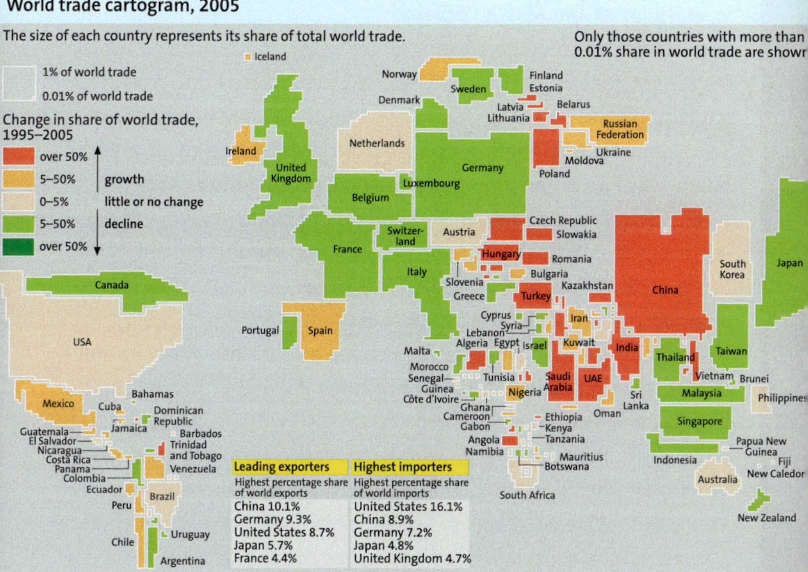

→ Focus on Vocab, pp. 69 ff.

Genetic Engineering

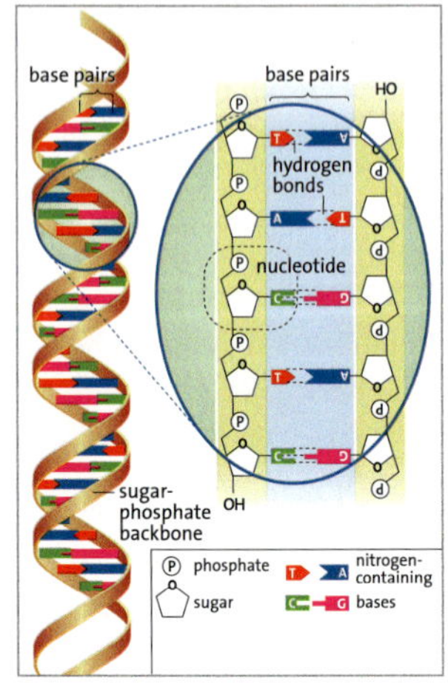

Genetic engineering (or genetic modification) is the **human manipulation of an organism's genetic material** to create a genetically modified organism that does not exist under natural conditions. During this process, new genetic material (DNA) is inserted into the host genome (= the entirety of an organism's hereditary information). First the **genetic material of interest is isolated and copied**, thereby generating a construct that contains all the necessary genetic elements, which is then **inserted into a host organism** in a second step.

Thus, **genetic engineering changes the genetic design or genetic blueprint of an organism** and **forms new combinations** of heritable (= *erblich*) genetic material. Although **stem cell research** and **cloning** are not considered to be genetic engineering by definition, these areas of scientific research are closely connected to genetic engineering because they can be used together.

In **medicine** genetic engineering is used e.g. for **the mass production of insulin, human growth hormones, follitism (for treating infertility) and vaccines**. Researchers are also working to genetically engineer humans and e.g. **replace defective humans genes with functional ones** and thus **cure genetic disorders and diseases** like Parkinson's disease, cancer, diabetes, heart diseases and arthritis.

Despite all the (possible) benefits of genetic engineering there are also **ethical concerns and criticism** that this technology is not only used for treatment but for enhancement, modification or alteration of a human being's character, behaviour, appearance, intelligence or adaptability.

Historical development

Year	Major scientific discovery or achievement
1856–63	Austrian monk and scientist **Gregor Johann Mendel** (1822–84) shows that the inheritance of certain traits follows particular laws (the **"Laws of Inheritance"**); he is considered to be the "father of modern genetics"
1953	American zoologist **James Watson** and British physicist **Francis Crick discover the double helix**, the chemical structure of DNA which makes up genes
1972	American biochemist **Paul Berg creates the first recombinant** (= altered, modified) **DNA**
1974	German biologist **Rudolf Jaenisch creates a transgenic mouse** by inserting foreign DNA into its embryo
1976	Genetic Engineering Technology Inc. (Genentech Inc.), **the first biotechnology company, is founded in California** by US businessman Robert A. Swanson and biochemist Dr. Herbert Boyer
1978	Genentech Inc. **produces genetically engineered human insulin**
1980	the **US Supreme Court rules that genetically altered life can be patented**
1986	first field trials in the **USA and France: genetically engineered tobacco plants** are resistant to herbicides (= *Unkrautvernichtungsmittel*)
1992	**China commercializes virus-resistant tobacco plants**
1994	the **first genetically-modified tomato**, designed to have a longer shell life, is released
June 2000	President Clinton announces **the completion of the first draft of the human genome**
Feb 2001	first analyses of the public and private genome projects are published; the big discovery: **Humans have about 30,000 to 40,000 genes, hardly more than a common weed or worm**
April 2003	the **human genome is declared a finished product**; the announcement coincides with the 50th anniversary of the discovery of the double helix

→ Focus on Vocab, pp. 89 ff.

Drama and Theatre

Drama

A **drama or play** is written to be performed by **actors** in a theatre, in a film, on television or on the radio. Traditionally, a play is composed of **acts** (units that reflect main stages in the development of the action), which are further subdivided into **scenes** (= sequences of continuous, uninterrupted action). Modern plays may just present a sequence of scenes. More reduced forms are **one-act plays**. One of the basic elements of drama is **conflict between opposing characters (= protagonist/antagonist)**, or contrasting ideas, attitudes and interests. Conflict creates tension and **dramatic action**, which is unfolded in **dialogues** and/or **monologues**. Good dialogues or monologues must capture the personalities, social positions, attitudes, thoughts and emotions of the characters. **Stage directions** given by the **author/playwright** help the director and the actors perform the play on stage. Such directions may be rather short and leave room for individual interpretation, while others are very detailed and indicate the precise design and arrangement of the **setting** (= time and place), **scenery**, **props** (= properties, i.e. furniture, decoration, etc.), the characters' appearances, movements, gestures, ways of speaking, or the **sound and lighting** to be used.

Drama is the generic term for the genre. The most important subclasses are:

- the **traditional tragedy**, which develops dramatic action like this:

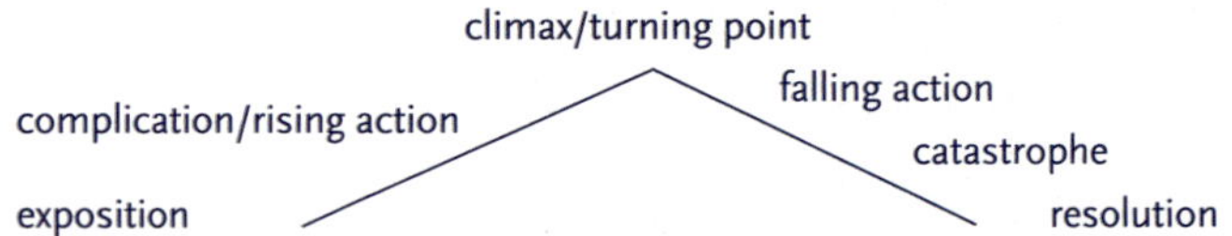

- the **traditional comedy**, which develops dramatic action like this:

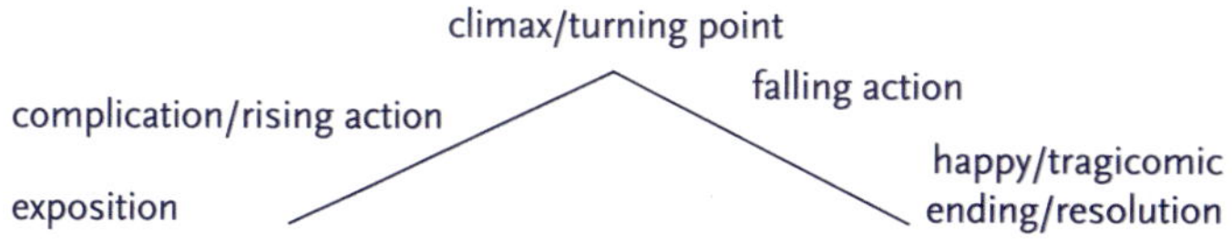

Theatre

Here are some of the important elements of a theatrical stage:

Cross-section view of the inside of the former Globe Theatre in London

Analysis of a Fictional Text

The 3 basic types of fictional texts

a) **Narrative texts** (e.g. novel, short story, fable)
b) **Dramatic texts** (e.g. drama/play, screenplay/script)
c) **Poetry/lyrics**

Step 1: Analysis of the general meaning

- Identify and specify the type of text as well as the theme/topic/subject of the given text.
- Answer the W-questions: who, what, where, when, why?
- Write a summary of the given text of about 150–200 words at the most.
- Identify the narrator and specify what point of view is being used to tell the story.
- Develop a first (general) evaluation of the meaning and message of the text.

Step 2: Analysis of basic elements

a) **Identify the structural and narrative/stylistic devices** and show **what effect and function** they have.

The following grid contains some terminology and tips for your analysis. The most relevant vocabulary can be found in the *Glossary of Literary Terms* in your Students' Book, pp. 339 ff.

Narrator, narrative situation, point of view, mode of presentation	first-person narrator, witness/observer narrator, third-person narrator, objective/reliable narrator, subjective/unreliable narrator, limited point of view, unlimited/omniscient point of view, panoramic presentation, scenic presentation, relation of acting time and narrating time

Structure	• (How) is the text structured? • What timespan does the narration cover? • What is the relation between acting time and narrating time ? • Which conflict is the story based on? • How does the action develop – or stagnate? • Are there any leitmotifs?
Characters	flat/round characters, protagonist vs. antagonist, minor character(s), hero(ine), antihero, outward appearance, behaviour, relationship to other characters, direct or indirect characterization
Setting (= time and place)	scenery, mental climate, basic mood, social environment, atmosphere • Does the scenery/setting itself imply any symbolism? (e.g. thunderstorm = danger, large city = liveliness, anonymity, etc.) • What is the effect on the audience? • What intention might the author/playwright have had?
Language/ style	level of speech, manner of speaking, style, syntax, choice of words, inner monologue, chain of associations, stream of consciousness, register

b) Never forget to quote from the text to demonstrate the correctness and accuracy of your work.

Step 3: Comment on and evaluation of the text

- Classify and evaluate the text and its message.
- Relate the given text to other texts of the same epoch/time and/or compare it with other texts by the same author that you have dealt with. Pay attention to striking similarities and/or differences.
- Critically comment on the text and finish with a concluding sentence.

Analysis of a Non-Fictional Text

Step 1: Analysis of structure and content

- Identify and specify the theme/topic/subject* of the given text.
- Identify the characteristics of the heading* (e.g. provocative, ironical, funny, etc.).
- Divide the text into parts and relate these parts to the heading and the whole text.
- Write a summary of 150 words at most.
- Determine the message of the text. Predict the basic characteristics of the text (type).
- Clarify the line of argument, the train of thought* (general structure of the text).

Step 2: Analysis of stylistic devices/use of language

a) **Identify the stylistic devices** and show their effect and function. The following grid contains vocabulary for your analysis. Most relevant vocabulary (marked with *) can be found in the *Glossary of Literary Terms* in your Students' Book, pp. 339 ff.

Register (= *Sprachebene*)	slang, colloquial, everyday English, written language, (in)formal, poetic, sophisticated, familiar, technical terms, scientific, religious, metaphorical
Choice of words	denotations*, connotations*, keywords, figurative*/literal meaning of words, emphatic/negative function of words, euphemisms*, synonyms*, abstractions
Style	plain, sober, natural, matter-of-fact, clear, precise, concise, vigorous, fluent, passionate, elegant, artificial, stilted, wordy, colourless, cliché-ridden, snappy, lengthy, clumsy, spontaneous, trite, expressing doubt/certainty
Tone	humorous, playful, colloquial, conciliatory, depressive, serious, solemn, ironical, satirical, sarcastic, warm-hearted, aggressive, whining, reproachful
Rhetorical devices	alliteration*, anaphora*, allusion*, reference*, antithesis*, ellipsis*, hyperbole*, irony*, metaphor*,

Rhetorical devices	paradox*, personification*, simile*, symbol*, understatement, exaggeration*, parallelism*, employment of leitmotifs*, repetitions*, juxtapositions*, (rhetorical) questions*, quotations, enumerations*, appeals, comparisons, digressions from the main topic, grammatical tenses, illustrations, superlatives, personal pronouns (we – they, I – you, our – their, us – them)

b) **Don't forget to include quotes** to demonstrate the correctness and accuracy of your work. This is ow to do it:

- When **referring** to an important part of the text without quoting the words, give the page(s) and/or line(s): e.g. Clinton tells the audience about his jogging with foreign students (ll. 15–19).
- You can **integrate the quotation** into your sentence: e.g. Clinton is determined to establish "an environment of lifelong learning" (l. 54), which means that ...
- You can **use a full quotation**: e.g. Clinton starts with the most important point: "First, to help every child begin school healthy and ready to learn." (l. 42).
- Note the abbreviations:
  - one page or line: p. 5/l. 5
  - more pages or lines: pp. 2–5/ll. 2–5
  - the following page(s), line(s): f./ff. (e.g. pp. 5f. or ll. 10ff.)

  Note: **Omissions** of any kind are indicated by [...]. Remarks or **changes from the original text** are indicated by squared brackets: *He* [Clinton] *says* ...

Step 3: Evaluation of the text

- State whether (or not) the text is well-structured/convincing/effective/appropriate ...
- Discuss if/to what extent the text/author is able to address the reader(ship).
- Critically comment on the text, and refer to similar texts that you have dealt with.
- Finish with a concluding sentence.

Analysis of Poetry and Lyrics/Songs

Poetry (from the Greek "poiesis" = making, creating) is a type of literature in which ideas, experiences and feelings are expressed in compact, imaginative, and often musical language. Poets arrange words in ways designed to touch readers' senses, emotions and minds. Lyrics are a set of words that accompany music, either by speaking or singing. The word *lyric* derives from the Greek word "lyrikos" (= a song sung by the lyre). Most poems and lyrics are written in lines that may contain patterns of rhyme and rhythm to help convey their meaning. They often use figures of speech and imagery to appeal to the readers' and listeners' emotions and imagination. The poet or songwriter usually invents a speaker from whose point of view the feelings, ideas, experiences, etc. are expressed. Poems and songs may be divided into stanzas (groups of lines) or sections and can greatly vary in structure, theme and atmosphere.

General meaning/ content	• What situation/topic is presented? • What is the theme; are there any (striking) leitmotifs? • What is the author's/singer's intention; what is the message of the poem/song? • What kind of register of English has been chosen (poetic, colloquial, archaic, slang, etc.)? • What is the melody like (harmonious, rhythmical, tuneful, staccato, etc.)?
Formal analysis: a) structural devices	• Examine – the structure of the poem/song (stanzas, lines, (lack of) punctuation, refrain(s), break(s), enjambements, chorus, etc.) – the use of repetitions and/or enumerations/parallelisms – the use of contrast(s)/antithesis – the use of an illustration (= an example to make an idea clear) – the rhyme scheme (e.g. pair rhyme aa bb cc; cross rhyme abab; enclosed rhyme abba) – the use of free verse

b) sense devices	– (How) are objects and ideas/thoughts brought together? – What type(s) of sentence(s) is/are used (hypotactical/paratactical sentences, questions, commands, etc.)? – Are there allusions/references to a certain topic (e. g. nature, city, love, etc.)? – Check on the use of simile (a direct comparison: "like, as"), metaphor (an implied comparison without a connective word: "an ocean of tears"), personifications (something nonhuman is given human characteristics: "the frosty cliffs looked cold"), or symbols (an object that also stands for some abstract idea: a red rose ➔ symbol of love, beauty). – the use of grammatical tenses – the speaker's point of view – the employment of hyperbole/exaggeration
c) sound devices	• Examine – the use of alliteration/anaphora – the use of rhymes and/or assonances (= imperfect rhymes) – the use of a particular rhythm, beat – the use of onomatopoeia (= words that imitate a sound: buzz, cuckoo, etc.) – the instrumentation, beat, vocal/instrumental type of music, vocals, etc. **➔ Show how these devices support, stress/emphasize the meaning/content of the poem/song (➔ function/effect).** **➔ Show how style and content are connected.** **➔ Show how sound and lyrics match and support each other.**
d) Final comment and evaluation	• Try to classify the given poem/song (refer to other poems/songs by the same author or authors of the same background). • Evaluate the poem/song (Is the poem/song convincing? Has the author/singer succeeded in conveying his/her message? etc.). • What do you consider to be the final message of the poem/song? • What do you consider to be the effect on the reader/listener?

Analysis of a Political Speech

General aspects of political rhetoric

The purpose of most political speeches is persuasion rather than information. There is always a (hidden, underlying) message involved, often related to certain attitudes and values of the speaker. A political statement intends to affect the listeners by making use of diverse structural and rhetorical devices. In order to understand and to be able to evaluate a political speech, one should consider the following aspects:

First (general) impression:	• topic, subject matter, general tone, issues and purpose of the speech
Contents and structure:	• salient and striking topics, important aspects • organization of the text, arrangement of parts (e.g. introduction, main part or body, conclusion) • train of thought, composition, line of argument
Circumstances of the speech/ political context:	• time and place/medium (e.g. TV, radio, face-to-face, Internet) • position of the speaker (president, leader of a political party, leader of a protest movement, etc.) • audience (mass audience, a limited group of people) • occasion (election campaign, protest demonstration, political debate, informal gathering) • genre and type (presidential address to the nation, sermon, speech at a demonstration, campus speech, testimony)

Formal and stylistic devices:	
a) language	• keywords and phrases • word groups/clusters related to a certain topic • different registers for different addressees (e. g. sophisticated language to address rich and/or educated people, use of dialect, etc.) • choice of words (colloquialisms, slang expressions, poetic expressions)
b) grammar	• sentence structure/syntax (use of main-/sub-clauses) • use of grammatical tenses (indirect references to history, future, etc.)
c) rhetoric	• use of rhetorical questions and answers • use of contrast and oppositions (positive/negative, familiar/alien, near/distant, etc.) • use of key symbols, slogans, stereotypes • abstractions and generalizations • use of grammatical persons (I, us, we – you, they: patterns of identification and solidarity or vice versa) • metaphors, personifications • allusions and references to history (American Dream, important political/historical issues, good/bad times, tradition, future, etc.); quotations • repetitions (alliterations, anaphora); parallelisms • comparisons, numbers, factual information • irony, exaggerations, simplifications • imperatives, emotionally-loaded words • concentration on essential points vs. wordy • insertions
d) manner of speaking/voice	• volume, tempo, stress, intonation, abrupt changes, pauses, rhythm
Evaluation:	→ Comment on the personal integrity of the speaker, the general political circumstances, the impact on the listeners. → Compare the speech/speaker to other political speeches/speakers. Was he/she convincing?

Basic Types of Fictional Texts

1. Narrative texts	**a) Novels** • are an extended and complex work of fiction written in prose. • contain a variety of characters, action and a greater complication of plot. • present a sustained exploration of the milieu, the characters, their motives. • can vary greatly in form, style and content; one less complex form is the novella (e.g. John Steinbeck, Of *Mice and Men* or *Cannery Row*). • have certain subclasses, e.g. the social novel (e.g. Harriet Beecher-Stowe, *Uncle Tom's Cabin*), the coming-of-age story (e.g. Mark Twain, *Tom Sawyer and Huckleberry Finn*, Paul Auster, *Moon Palace*). **b) Short stories** • are written in prose and are shorter and less complex than a novel. • are mostly confined to one setting, a limited number of characters and events. • often employ an open plot with an abrupt opening and ending. • do not put focus on the development of a character but on a significant incident or decisive moment that reveals strengths and weaknesses of characters, mostly presented as a snapshot of life. • are told from the point of view of a narrator who is created by the autor. • place maximum significance on the few things mentioned, which are aimed at producing a certain effect on the reader's mind. • emerged in the USA in the 19th century in response to the development of the newspapers, which required shorter forms of text; Edgar Allan Poe (1809–1849) is often regarded as the originator of the short story; other famous writers of short stories include Ernest Hemingway, Annie Proulx, and T.C. Boyle. **c) Fables** • are a short text in which animals represent human types (➔ the beast fable).

1. Narrative texts	• are a form of allegory exemplifying an abstract moral thesis or principle of human behaviour. • are didactic and are intended to teach the reader a moral lesson. • Two famous writers of fables are James Thurber and George Orwell.
2. Dramatic texts	a) **Dramas/plays** • are any work designed for performance in a theater. • require actors/actresses who take on the roles of different characters, performing the actions and speaking the dialogue or monologue. • mostly contain stage directions included by the playwright, telling the actors how and where to move on stage as well as giving information about how to arrange the stage, what props, sound effects or lighting to use. → Focus on Facts, Drama and Theatre, pp. 152 f. b) **Screenplays/scripts** • are a written work, especially for a film or a television programme. • consist of numbered scenes which show action and dialogue descriptions. • have numbered slug lines telling the reader that the story has changed in location and time (e. g. INT. WAREHOUSE – NIGHT; EXT. STREET – DAY)
3. Poetry/ lyrics	a) **Poetry** • is a type of literature that is not prose, in which ideas, experiences and feelings are expressed in compact, imaginative and often musical language. • may be arranged in lines and may contain patterns of rhyme/rhythm. • often contains figures of speech and imagery to appeal to the readers' and listeners' emotions and imagination. b) **Lyrics** • are a set of words that accompany music, either spoken or sung. → Focus on Skills, Analysis of Poetry and Lyrics/Songs, pp. 158 f.

Basic Types of Non-Fictional Texts

The 4 basic types of non-fictional texts

1. Descriptive texts: the author wants to inform in a relatively balanced and neutral way (e. g. description of a landscape, a place, a person, an object ...)

2. Narrative texts: the author wants to inform the reader about a development or a sequence of events; the report (objectively or subjectively) gives answers to the questions *who? what? where? when? why?* and *how?* and often presents further details. Reports* are often made livelier by fictional elements, e. g. a detailed description of people or the way people are affected by an event, etc. (e. g. travel report, report on the development of a situation ...)

3. Expository texts: complicated and difficult facts are presented and explained in a matter-of-fact way; the structure pattern of such texts is called **topical order** (= a sequence of points follows a statement of the topic at the beginning of the text (e. g. explanatory notes, scientific reports, factual texts, descriptions of historical events ...)

4. Argumentative texts: the author tries to influence the reader directly; this text type tends to be more critical and appellative, using persuasive arguments (e. g. commentary, criticism, review*, essay*, sermon*, pamphlet, political speech* ...); these texts mostly deal with controversial topics; reasons are advanced for and/or against the matter and are arranged in a well-planned order

Forms of argumentative texts

Structure	Type 1	Type 2	Type 3
Introduction	Presenting a topic and giving opinions on the problem	Presenting a topic and giving opinions on the problem	Presenting a topic and giving opinions on the problem
↓	**arguments** ↓	**arguments** ↓	**arguments** ↓
Main part	supporting facts	counter-arguments and refutation to stress the author's position	argument → counter-argument argument → counter-argument argument → counter-argument, etc. [mainly used in disputes and debates]
↓	↓	↓	↓
Conclusion	Conclusion	Conclusion	Conclusion

A non-fictional text* that puts forth a personal view has a **unity of thought**, and usually follows a clear structure (line of thoughts*, train of thought*, line of argument*).

Here are some of the most common **compositional patterns for structuring texts**:

Listing structure:	**Method:** Enumerating, numbering of facts, ideas, arguments **Effect:** Clarity and coherence through parallel arrangement
Progressive structure:	**Method:** Using a clearly-defined starting point; developing on a cause-to-effect or problem-solution arrangement **Effect:** Clarity through unity and logical coherence
Antithetical structure:	**Method:** Contrasting and juxtaposing of facts, ideas and arguments **Effect:** Clarity and emphasis through comparison and contrast

Characterization of a Figure in Literature

Fictional characters can be presented in a number of ways. In general, a character in a fictional text is developed through action, description, language and ways of speaking.

Types of characters

Relevance within the text and characteristics	
• **protagonist** (the main character around whom most of the work revolves)	• **major characters** (main characters who dominate the story)
• **antagonist** (the person who the protagonist is against; often the villain)	• **minor characters** (less important persons who support the main character(s) by letting them interact or reveal their personalities, etc.)
• **the modern hero** (the average man/woman)	• **dynamic character** (changing and developing, with different traits)
• **the anti-hero** (often dishonest, graceless or inept person who struggles in life; the loser)	• **static characters** (unchanging, often stereotypical)
• **the tragic hero** (e.g. Macbeth; person who ends tragically as a result of personal flaws)	• **round character** (three-dimensional, with different and changing facets to the personality)
• **romantic hero** (a character with a strong will and personality who goes against established norms; often this figure experiences melancholy, isolation and unfulfilled and unhappy love)	• **flat character** (one-dimensional, viewed only from one side, often stereotypical)
• **the Hemingway hero** (a character who has been at war, drinks too much, the loner, "cowboy")	

Types of characterization in literature

- In a **direct characterization of a character** the narrator or one of the other characters **tells** the readers/audience what the character's personality is like.
- In an **indirect characterization** the writer **shows/presents** the character talking and acting which reveals the character's personality. Indirect characterization can be achieved through:
  a) **Speech** (What does the character say, how does he/she communicate and interact with others?)
  b) **Thoughts** (What is revealed through the person's private thoughts, e.g. in a monologue, soliloquy, a diary entry, etc.?)
  c) **Effect on others/on the character** (How does the person react/respond to others? Does he/she have any relationships? How do others react to the person?)
  d) **Actions** (What does the person do, how does he/she behave?)
  e) **Looks** (appearance, body language, gestures, facial expression, etc.)

How to write a literary characterization

Step 1: Collect the facts and clues given in the text and move from the outward features and characteristics to the inward nature of the character:

- **personal data** (name, age, sex, nationality)
- **outward appearance** (body, face, clothes, etc.)
- **attitudes/views** (thoughts, dreams, emotions)
- **behaviour** (toward other characters, actions)
- **relationships** (social background, family, friends)

Step 2: Draw your conclusions about the person's character and relate your findings to the text by referring to specific lines. Use the simple present for your characterization.

Step 3: Follow the introduction – main part – conclusion pattern in your characterization. Write an introductory sentence that answers the w-questions.

Writing a Comment and a Review

A Comment

A written comment expresses your personal opinion on a certain topic or issue. It is a common means used in print media in order to state one's opinion to the readership in a more or less critical way. Take some notes first, and structure your thoughts systematically before starting to write.

1. Introduction

- Make some introductory remarks in which you, for example, raise a question, refer to a current problem, etc.
- The introduction should clarify your topic/concern.

2. Main part – arguments

- State, demonstrate and describe the positive and negative effects of a topic/situation.
- Support your view of the situation by giving examples. You can, for example, refer to or quote famous people or experts on this matter, or relate it to other comparable issues.
- Emphasize the argument by referring to further/future consequences.

3. Conclusion

- Conclude your comment by giving your personal view of the situation/problem.
- Strategically, it is smart to relate your final remarks to your introduction in order to finally "wrap up" the topic and make your point.

A Review of a Fiction Book or Film

Step 1: Plot*/characters*/theme*

- Briefly summarize the plot of the book/the film (approx. 150 words). ("Who/where/when/what/why"-questions should be answered.)

- Include the type of film (e.g. feature film*, western)/book (e.g. historical novel), title, author/director, publishing/release year, edition, special features.
- Briefly describe the main characters* and how they are related.
- Briefly outline the basic theme(s) and leitmotif(s)* of the book/the film.
- Describe the overall atmosphere of the book/the film.

Step 2: Narrative/cinematic aspects

- Point out striking narrative qualities (e.g. point of view*, metaphorical language, structure of the plot*).
- Refer to any striking cinematic devices that create/reinforce the atmosphere of the film.
- Mention which actors were chosen for the respective roles.
- Explain what the book's/the film's message and the author's/director's intention may be.

Step 3: Evaluation

- Say what you like or dislike about: the plot, the structure, the directing, the camera work, the sound, special effects, the casting, the performance of the actors.
- Explain whether the book/the film has successfully conveyed any/its main message.
- Comment on the actors: Have they successfully personified and typified the characters?
- Consider and quantify shortcomings/weaknesses and strengths of the book/the film.
- If the film is a literary adaptation: How well has the story been adapted? – Is there anything missing (in comparison to the novel)? – or in comparison to other books/films by the same author/director?

Step 4: Conclusion

- Is the film worth viewing?/Is the book worth reading?
- Would you recommend the book/the film? – What was your favourite part of the book/film?

Writing – Summary/Essay/Creative Writing

Summary

A summary ...

- gives the most relevant facts and the overall meaning of a text,
- must not contain your own thoughts and opinions,
- begins with an introductory sentence (name of the author, type of text, title, topic/problem the text deals with, basic matters of the text, year of publication),
- is about 150–200 words long, depending on the length of the text that is to be summed up,
- does not contain direct speech or quotations (instead uses reported speech and/or paraphrasing),
- should be factual,
- leaves out irrelevant details,
- should basically be written in the present tense,
- should present the events in chronological order (➔ no suspense),
- closes with a sentence that sums up the main message of the text and its intention.

Essay (= literary appreciation)

An essay ...

- is a type of text that is written in a **defined structure**:
  a) **statement** (➔ of the main idea),
  b) **development** (➔ proving the statement by reference to facts, examples, etc.),
  c) **conclusion** (➔ the main idea is re-stated),
- often makes **use of contrast** (i.e. contrasts are employed to give more force to the main idea),
- contains **illustrations** (e.g. experiences, examples from everyday life, an anecdote, a description, etc.) to arouse the interest of the reader,

- employs stylistic and rhetorical devices to emphasize certain aspects and to influence the reader,
- has a distinctive line of argument/train of thought → a clear argumentative structure.

Creative writing

Before you start writing a text, you **should collect ideas** about:
- the topic/the main idea (what?),
- main characters/constellation of characters (who?),
- the setting (where? and when?),
- the plot (= development of action → in what way?),
- the genre of your story (romance, comedy, thriller, tragedy),
- the atmosphere (joyful, ghostly, cold, scary, etc.).

→ Give your text a **clear structure**: beginning – main part – ending.
→ Put your ideas in an understandable order.
→ Decide on which grammatical tense you want to use for your story (present – past – future).

Vocabulary and Phrases for Text Analysis

When you are asked to analyse and interpret a text, you should express yourself precisely and appropriately. Therefore, it is important to use a specific terminology that employs **technical terms** (e.g. stylistic devices) and a variety of formulations that make your text more fluent and less repetitive.
The following words and phrases are related to the most relevant aspects.

Introduction	The author
• The text deals with/is about … • The theme of the text is … • The text is composed of/consists of … • Three/two … different parts can be distinguished … • The first part runs from line … to line … • At the beginning of the text, … • The author begins by saying … • At the end of the text,/Finally,/Lastly, … • The first part forms the introduction … • The main/central/principal idea is … • In the conclusion, the author states that … • In the final part, the author …	• The author thinks/says/believes that … • According to the author, …/In his/her view … • The author illustrates his/her point of view with … • The author makes a comment on … • The author is convinced that … • The author's judgements are (un)realistic/not objective/unfounded/well-founded … • The reader can sympathize with the author's view on … • The author expresses doubts/questions … • The author makes remarks on … • The intention/aim/objective of the author is … • The author portrays believable characters. • The author gives a detailed/vague description of …

The text/the plot/the story	The characters
• The story is told from the perspective of ... • The plot is set in ... • The text is written in an ironical tone. • The text contains comical elements. • The setting of the action is unreal/imaginary. • The action becomes more/less intense ... • The situation seems quite absurd... • Suspense is created because/by ... • The ending of the story is believable ...	• The main/principal character in the story is ... • The author characterizes him/her as ... • He has many positive traits ... • His behaviour is marked by ... • Another essential quality is ... • She shows her superiority by saying that ... • He is characterized as ... • The protagonist lacks ... • As far as his outward appearance is concerned, ... • She plays an important/a secondary role ...
The structure	**The action**
• The exposition gives information about ... • The first scene introduces ... • The starting point for the action is ... • The conflict reaches its climax in ... • The turning point is indicated by ... • The crisis is in scene ... • In the last scene, ... • This play/story has a happy/tragic ending.	• The action takes place in ... • The action develops in ... stages ... • The action progresses fast ... • The scene contains a flashback. • The action is interrupted by ... • This is one of the central scenes ... • The development of the action is slowed down by ...

Purpose (of texts)	Vocabulary
• The author wants to arouse the reader's interest. • The text appeals to ... • He tries to manipulate ... • He/She wants the reader to become aware of ... • The text addresses young/poor/... people ... • It is the author's objective to create a feeling of ... • The author attempts to influence the reader. • The advert suggests to the reader that ...	• The vocabulary contains many colloquial expressions/technical terms ... • This word/term expresses fear ... • This word has a negative meaning/negative associations ... • This phrase suggests ... • These phrases belong to the spoken language. • The choice of words gives the text its romantic/technical/... character. • These expressions are typical of ...

Criticizing the author	Further useful expressions
• I (dis-)agree with the author on ... • I don't understand why he/she ... • I consider it to be wrong/difficult to ... • This ... cannot be taken seriously ... • I'd like to comment on ... • It has to be pointed out that ... • This statement contradicts his view of ... • There is a contradiction in ... • It goes without saying that ... • It is essential that ... • This raises the question as to why he/she ... • What really matters is ... • This problem has nothing to do with ... • This is of no importance/significance for ...	• To give an explanation for ... • The author pretends to know ... • The author describes the characteristics of ... • The article is based on ... • The author makes an allusion to ... • This sentence reveals the true character of ... • He/She appeals to emotions rather than ... • He quotes some experts as an example of ... • The article relates ... to ... • The text conveys the impression that ... • The writer establishes a relationship between ... • The author's theses are ... • He supports his thesis with ... • His/Her outlook on life is ...

Criticizing the author	Further useful expressions
• As far as ... is concerned, ... • From this point of view, ... • Generally speaking, ... • As a matter of fact, ... • In theory, ..., but in reality, ...	• He takes a positive/negative view of ... • The author generalizes about ... • This is a great simplification of ...

→ When you analyse or interpret a text, you should use **Standard English**.

→ You should generally use the **present tense** when you describe/explain or analyse specific aspects of the text.

→ Be careful not to imitate the tone or the language of the text – when you write about a text written in colloquial English, you still have to use Standard English in order to appear **impersonal and objective**.

→ Try to **vary the beginnings of your sentences** by employing different connectives.

→ Even when you express your personal opinion about a text/the author, etc., your choice of words should be appropriate and respectful. It can be helpful not to begin sentences with "I ..." or "I think ..." but to **focus on the text, the author**, etc. (e.g. The article gives the impression that ..., The author seems to intend to ...). This appears much more impersonal and academic.

→ **Don't overdo it by being too formal** or stilted – your text should reflect your view and stance on the matter.

Note: Explanations of the respective technical terms can be found in the *Glossary of Literary Terms*, SB, pp. 339 ff.